LINUX

in ea

CW00692522

David Nash

COMPUTER
STEP

In easy steps is an imprint of Computer Step
Southfield Road . Southam
Warwickshire CV33 OFB . England

Tel: 01926 817999 Fax: 01926 817005
http://www.computerstep.com

Notice of Liability
Every effort has been made to ensure that this book contains accurate
and current information. However, Computer Step and the author shall
not be liable for any loss or damage suffered by readers as a result of
any information contained herein.

Trademarks
All trademarks are acknowledged as belonging to their respective
companies.

Printed and bound in the United Kingdom

ISBN 1-84078-072-X

Contents

Introducing Linux

This chapter gives you a basic introduction to Linux.
You'll learn what Linux is, why you might want to use it,
and a little about its history. You will also find out how to
enter commands, run programs, how to find your way
around Linux disks and perform common operations on
files.

Covers

Chapter One

What is Linux?

Linux is an operating system for computers, just like MS-DOS, Windows and MacOS. Linux belongs to the Unix family of operating systems, a powerful type of system not found on home computers before Linux came along.

Linux, however, can be used for many different purposes: at home for games, at work, on desktop workstations or on network servers. There is even a car stereo that plays digital music files and that runs on Linux too.

Linux is pronounced with a short 'i', something like "Linn-Ucks."

The big thing about Linux is that it is *free software*. This means two things: firstly it means that you don't have to pay for it and secondly that you can have complete access to the source code of Linux. You may then copy it, alter it and redistribute it to anyone else if you want. The only condition is that the source must remain freely available to all.

Although by the terms of the licence, no-one can charge for Linux, you will have to pay for distribution. This could be on a plain CD-ROM, in a box with a manual or via the Internet. The charge for distribution will vary accordingly and in the latter case will be only telephone and Internet access fees (if any). Linux people like to say, "think free speech, not free beer."

www.linux .org contains a wealth of information and links about every aspect of Linux distributions, Applications, Hardware, User Groups and more.

This freedom means that Linux has a great deal of support from people all over the world who collaborate in it's development and keep in touch via the Internet. As a result Linux has most of the features of any other PC operating system and in many cases outperforms its commercial rivals. Linux is known for its stability, meaning that it very rarely 'crashes' or needs to be rebooted, even when installing new software.

When bugs are occasionally found, the open source community has an excellent record of responding quickly. Linux fixes are usually released within days, sometimes within hours, of a bug being discovered.

History

Linux was developed in 1991 by a student at the university of Helsinki by the name of Linus Torvalds.

He was dissatisfied with the facilities that were available to him in the university and decided it would be fun to write an operating system for himself. When he had something vaguely recognisable, he released it to a small group of enthusiasts known to him on the Internet. This group assisted Linus and contributed modifications and new features until the kernel of the operating system was working.

www. linuxhq .org is the place to go to get the latest on the Linux kernel releases. It also has links to the latest kernel files for download.

The kernel of the operating system is the central core of the system, which interacts with the computer and provides services for the user and application programs to use. Around this kernel are many other programs providing most of the commands available in Linux.

In Linux, these programs have mostly come from the GNU project. This aims to produce a completely free operating system based on the same principles as, and compatible with, the Unix operating system. GNU programs are all released under a licence called the **GNU Public Licence**, which describes the principles of free, open source software. It does not permit software covered by it to be reused, except as part of another package also covered by the GPL. In this way GNU software remains free.

freshmeat. net has all the latest software releases for Linux. It is updated throughout the day and has a members' section and searchable archives.

Since a number of the programs used with the Linux kernel are GNU programs, some people believe that the operating system should be generally known as GNU/Linux. Unfortunately for them the general public tends to shorten names not lengthen them, therefore it is unlikely that the term GNU/Linux will become popular.

In 1994 Linux was released as version 1.0. It had over 100,000 users by this time and has since become much better known. It is estimated that there are at present over 8 million users worldwide. With some of the biggest IT vendors now supporting Linux this number is sure to continue rising.

...cont'd

Linux is under constant development. In order to ensure that a stable version is always available for normal users, whilst maintaining the development of new functions and new additions which might make the kernel a little less reliable, Linux has a split version number model.

The kernel version number is displayed when you login to Linux.

Versions with an *even* minor version number (the 'o' in '1.0') are stable, whilst those with an *odd* minor version number (such as '1.1') are development or test versions of Linux.

At the time of writing, the most recent stable version is 2.2. The old 2.1 development branch of Linux was incorporated into the previous stable version 2.0.36, and the result was 2.2.0, with a new development branch (2.3) to be started. New stable versions incorporating fixes and enhancements are added as 2.2.1 etc. and radical new features begin their life in the 2.3.0, 2.3.1 versions, and so on.

Since version 1.0 Linux has had many extra features added by developers all over the world. Features such as:

Graphical environments
Providing windows and integrated desktops.

Networking
Providing interworking with the internet, other computers and with industry-standard platforms.

Multimedia capabilities
Sound, graphics and video.

Linux has improved to the extent that major players in the computer industry are starting to take notice. Many major database and office tools are now being developed for Linux. Linux has now truly come of age.

Installing Linux

Here we describe how to install Red Hat Linux, one of the most popular Linux distributions. Your version might differ but all the important concepts will be there.

Throughout the Red Hat install program, use Tab to move from field to field. Press Space to select an item, press Return when you have finished that screen and remember to read all the on-screen messages!

1 Insert the Red Hat CD-ROM and boot the PC from it. If you cannot boot from the CD, restart your computer in MSDOS mode, then go to the DOSUTILS directory on the CD-ROM and enter the following command:

```
autoboot
```

This will start the Linux install session.

2 Follow the on-screen prompts until you get to "installation class" and Select "Custom". This allows you to control the installation of Linux.

3 Select "Disk Druid" when asked. You will now have to choose a disk partition to hold your Linux installation.

See chapter three for more information about disks and partitions in Linux.

Disks and Partitions

A partition is like a logical disk, like C:, or D: in Windows. Normally you will have more drive letters than actual physical hard disks in your system. This is because the hard disk is partitioned into sections. In Linux the first hard disk is known as *hda* and the second as *hdb*. The partitions are numbered in sequence *hda1*, *hda2*, *hdb1*, and so on. Each physical disk will have one primary partition and a number of logical partitions. Windows calls the first primary partition on the first disk C:, the first primary partition on the second disk D: and so on through the disks. Next it gives letters in order to all the other partitions on the first disk, then on the second, and so on.

Because of this, changing the OS type to Linux on a partition can change your Windows drive letters. The best way to avoid this is to use the last logical partition on your system for Linux.

You can resize and add partitions using 3rd-party software, or use the freeware FIPS on the Linux CD.

4   In the Disk Druid screen press Return then Enter / (the slash character) next to the partition name you want to install Linux on:

Mount Point	Device	Requested	Actual	Type
/	hda3	500M	500M	Win95 FAT32

directory name   partition name

5   Now add other partitions you want to use. It is normal to reserve a small partition (less than 100 Megabytes) for "swap". Other directories which may have their own partition include /home and /usr.

Always back up your disks before resizing partitions in case of problems.

6   Next you will be asked about swap. If you don't have a partition for swap you can add a swap file later. Otherwise select the swap partition name.

7   Select the partitions just chosen so that they will be formatted for Linux files.

If you have the disk space choose the development packages anyway, as some Linux software is distributed as "source", which will require these utilities to be able to run it.

8   The default set of packages is now displayed. Remember to select printer support if you need to use a printer, and all the development packages if you might want to do any programming.

9   Now choose your mouse type. Remember to select "Emulate 3 Buttons" if your mouse only has two, as Linux needs three buttons. Next select your video card type. If yours is not listed try VGA or SVGA. The next stage is to choose your monitor. If you can't find yours you can try Generic or Generic Multisync. When asked, allow it to probe your video card.

...cont'd

Older versions of Linux with kernels less than 2.2.0, use the names "lp1" and "lp2" for LPT1 and LPT2 respectively.

10 Next you will be asked a range of questions about: using a LAN (Local Area Network), which timezone you are in and which services to start (the defaults should be adequate).

11 The next screen allows you to choose a printer. Remember Linux calls LPT1: "lp0" and LPT2 is called "lp1".

12 Now choose a root password. "Root" is the name of the superuser, used for all administrative tasks on Linux so this is very important. Don't forget it and don't tell anyone!

13 Now you have the option to make a bootdisk. It is recommended that you do so, as in an emergency it could be the only way you have of booting your Linux system.

14 Finally configure the boot loader, LILO. This is the most important step as it allows you to actually boot into your new Linux installation. You have the choice of placing LILO on the partition with Linux or on the Master Boot Record (on your Windows partition). The latter option is recommended as this partition is normally the boot partition.

If you do have an existing Windows partition make sure it is in the LILO configuration. You may want to set it to the default.

Logging in

When you start Linux you will see the login prompt. If this is the first time you are logging in the only user on the system will be the superuser, known as "root".

To log in

1 Enter your username at the login prompt.

```
Red Hat Linux version 5.2 (Apollo)

Kernel 2.2.2 on an i686

localhost Login: root
```

You won't see your password as you type it, so be careful to get it right!

2 Enter your password at the prompt.

```
password:
```

3 If you have entered the username and password correctly, you will find yourself at the Linux prompt.

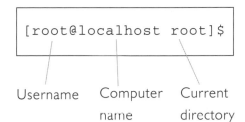

Username   Computer   Current
              name   directory

Adding a User

After you have logged in for the first time you need to add a user. To add a user "Fred" use the following command:

```
useradd -m fred
```

Setting a Password

You can now set the password for your user. Use this command:

```
passwd fred
```

To log out, just press Ctrl+D.

Entering Commands

 Linux provides several "virtual" consoles (normally six). This means that you can log in up to six times and run different programs on each virtual screen. Change from one virtual screen to another by pressing Ctrl+Alt+number. For example: Ctrl+Alt+2 to change to virtual console 2.

When you have logged in with your new username you will be placed at the shell prompt. The shell is the program which accepts your commands and which runs programs for you. We will learn more about the shell later.

The prompt will appear as a $ sign which, by default on RedHat Linux, is prefixed with your username, the name of your Linux machine and the current directory name.

There are two types of command you can enter at the shell prompt: Shell commands; and Programs.

Shell commands instruct the shell itself to do something. They are used for job control and control of how the shell operates and your environment. Typing a program name causes the shell to go and find that program on the hard disk and then run it.

Some shell commands are:

echo	Display text or other values on the screen
cd	Change current working directory
pwd	Print the current working directory on the screen

Some common programs are:

ls	List directory contents
cp	Copy Files
cat	Display the Contents of File(s)

We will learn more about all of these later.

Directories and the Filesystem

In common with other Unix systems and many other operating systems, Linux disks are organised into a logical tree structure formed of directories. Each directory is a container which can hold files (programs or data) and other directories. A directory held within a directory is sometimes known as a subdirectory. The base of the tree is known, not unreasonably, as the root. This is represented by the / (slash) symbol. The following diagram shows part of the Linux filesystem (starting from the root) and shows some common directories found within it:

Directories are sometimes called folders.

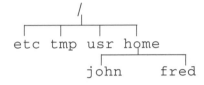

Some root level directories found on all Linux systems are:

/bin – contains executable programs ("binary" files) which make up the commands of the operating system.

/boot – contains files related to booting the system, including the Kernel image file itself (the core of the operating system which is loaded at boot time).

/dev – used for special files which represent devices on the system. Contained in this directory are files representing each hard disk and partition on the system, each serial and parallel port, mouse interface and all other devices.

/etc – this is a sort of "miscellaneous" directory which holds all kinds of files related to all kinds of things. Many system configuration files are in here such as the file which controls the X window server and local area network configuration files.

/home – contains the home directories of users on the system. That is, the directory a user finds himself in when he logs on, and in which he has full ownership permissions.

/lib – libraries (shared program files) used by programs and the operating system are in this directory.

/mnt – this is a general mounting point (see later).

/opt – contains optional files and packages loaded onto the system.

/proc – this is not a real directory, it is simulated by the operating system. It shows many pieces of information about the hardware and software of the system.

/root – the home directory of the superuser, "root".

/sbin – system binary files, i.e. executable programs which form part of the operating system.

/tmp – directory available to all users and programs for storing temporary files and data.

/usr – general directory containing several subdirectories with source code, executable programs, and whole application directories.

/var – this directory contains variable data like system logs, print spool files, and lock files.

The location of any file on the system can be represented by writing first the root symbol, followed by the name of each directory, representing the sub-branch of the tree where the file resides. These elements are separated by more / symbols.

For example: /home/fred/myfile.dat

This notation is called a path. The example represents the file "myfile.dat" in the subdirectory "fred", located in the root-level directory "home".

Linux filenames can be any length and are case sensitive. They can also contain spaces, although you may need to enclose the name in quotes (" and ") when you pass a filename to a command, so that the command knows that it is all one name.

This means that "myfile", "MyFile", and "MYFILE" are all different names and may coexist in the same directory.

Basic File Handling Commands

Directory Listing

As shown on the previous table, you can enter "ls" to see a list of files in your current directory. ls can be used with various options which affect the way it shows the list:

For example:

ls -l   Long listing, including file ownership, date and time, and access permissions

ls -a   Show all files, including hidden files (those whose name begins with a dot)

ls -t   Order the list by date and time instead of alphabetically

These options may be combined. Thus to show a long-style listing in date and time order, but reversed so the most recent files are at the end of the list, use:

```
ls -ltr
```

Copying and Moving files around

To copy files, use the cp command as follows:

```
cp myfile myfilecopy
```

The destination (the second filename given) can also be the name of a directory. In this case the file is copied to a new file of the same name in that directory.

To move a file from one location to another, use the mv command.

The following command:

```
mv myfile mysubdirectory
```

will move "myfile" into the subdirectory named "mysubdirectory".

...cont'd

The mv command is also used to rename files, for example:

```
mv myfile newname
```

This will change the name of the file "myfile" so that it is called "newname".

Deleting files

You can delete files permanently using the rm command (short for "remove"). For example:

```
rm oldfile
```

will permanently delete the file called "oldfile".

The "more" command is case-sensitive. Remember to press q not Q.

Displaying the contents of a text file

You can display the contents of a file with the "cat" command. This is short for *concatenate*, because the same command can be used to join files together.

```
cat myfile.txt
```

If the file is longer than one screen you can display it a page at a time with "more".

```
more longfile.txt
```

Press Space to show the next page. Press Return to show the next line and press "q" to quit and stop displaying the file.

Wildcards

When entering commands or running programs you sometimes want to specify a range of filenames, which the command should act on. An example would be "List all the files whose name begins with b". This is done by using "wildcard" characters in the filenames specified to the command. Each wildcard character matches many alternative characters.

    *   Matches any string of characters

    ?   Matches any single character

These characters are used in combination with normal characters. So to list all files whose name begins with "b", you could enter:

```
ls b*
```

What actually happens when you enter a wildcard filename is that the shell itself expands the wildcard, turning it into a list of matching filenames and passing the whole list to the command. If our directory contained two files beginning with "b", such as "bigfile.txt" and "beta1.dat", the above command would be invisibly changed to:

```
ls beta1.dat bigfile.txt
```

so the ls command shows just those two files. Since the wildcard expansion is done by the shell, we can use it for any commands we want to that will handle a list of files. We don't need to worry about whether the command itself will understand the wildcard notation.

For example, to copy all files from the /home/fred directory into the /home/john directory, enter the following:

```
cp /home/fred/* /home/john
```

This works because the cp command accepts a list of files on the command line and expects the last one to be a directory name in which to put them.

Finding Files

How can you find a file whose location you have forgotten? That is, you know it exists but don't know in which directory it is located. You could always visit each directory on the system in turn, and use the ls command in each. This would be very laborious and could take quite some time.

Fortunately there are a couple of commands available to help in this task.

The first one is called find. To find all files in a directory called "mydirectory" and all its subdirectories enter:

In the find command use a dot to mean the current directory, like this: find . -print

```
find mydirectory -print
```

To find a particular file, enter:

```
find mydirectory -print -name filename
```

To find all files matching a pattern you can use wildcards, but in this case we want to pass the wildcards to the find command, rather than let the shell expand them. This is because the shell only looks in one directory when expanding wildcards and, unless the files we are seeking are in the current directory, the expansion will not help us.

To pass wildcards directly to a command without letting the shell expand them, we can enclose them in single quotes 'like this'.

Only use the single quote or apostrophe (') for this.

So, to find all files beginning with 'b' in the current directory, and all subdirectories, use:

```
find . -print -name 'b*'
```

The Locate Command

There is a faster way to find files than using the find command, which is a rather *brute force* method. The find command can take some time to search the filesystem, particularly if you have a lot of files and directories. This is because it visits every directory and subdirectory in turn to see if the files you want are there.

A faster way is to use the "locate" command. This command searches a ready-built index in order to locate files rapidly. Locate searches partial filenames by default so wildcards are unnecessary.

To find all files containing the word "big":

```
locate big
```

Of course nothing comes for free and the catch is that you have to build the index which locate uses to find files. There is another command used for this, called "updatedb".

To generate the index simply enter:

```
updatedb
```

on a line on it's own. The command will take a little while as it searches the filesystem and builds it's database, but once done the locate command will find files much quicker than using find.

Make sure you are logged in as root, or the superuser, when you run the updatedb command, otherwise there will be some directories which cannot be scanned because you do not have permission.

Users, Groups and Privileges

This chapter teaches you about users and ownership of files. You will learn about adding users and groups, and find out how to change the ownership and permissions for accessing files.

Covers

Chapter Two

File Ownership

In Linux each file is owned by a user, normally the user who created it. The owner of a file has the right to read the file, run it if it is a program file and to change or delete the file. Other users can do only those things for which the owner has given permission.

A file also belongs to a named group. Each user on the system is a member of one or more groups. Users who are members of the group to which a given file belongs can be given special permission to read, write or run a file.

To see file ownership details

1 Use the ls command with the "-l" option to list files.

```
ls -l /etc
```

2 The listing shows permissions, file owner and group.

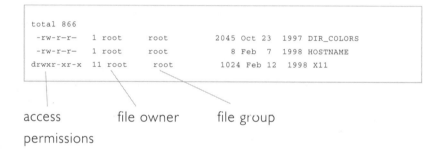

```
total 866
-rw-r-r—   1 root      root        2045 Oct 23  1997 DIR_COLORS
-rw-r-r—   1 root      root           8 Feb  7  1998 HOSTNAME
drwxr-xr-x 11 root     root        1024 Feb 12  1998 X11
```

access
permissions

file owner

file group

To change the owner of a file
Use the "chown" command:

```
chown username filename
```

To change the group of a file
Use the "chgrp" command:

```
chgrp groupname filename
```

Permissions

Access permissions for a file are divided into three:

1. Permissions for the file's owner.

2. Permissions for members of the file's group.

3. Permissions for everyone else ("others").

Each of these three sets of users may be given, or refused, the right to read the file, to change or delete the file, or to execute the file.

So, there are nine possible permissions which can be given or refused in combination. They are written as a string of nine characters:

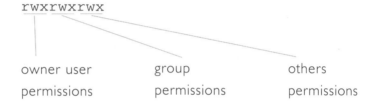

To give, or take away, a permission
Use the command "chmod" (change mode):

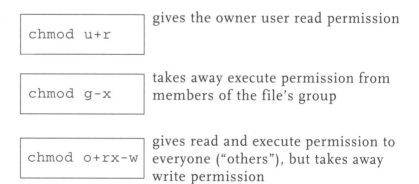

If you omit the scope ("u", "g", or "o") the permission given will apply to all three groups.

...cont'd

Sometimes the permission information is changed to a number. This works like this:

Each of the three "rwx" parts is taken as a binary number. A "1" means the permission is given, a "0" means it is not given.

For example, "101" would represent read and execute permission.

 The following binary numbers equal these decimal digits:

The three binary numbers (one for User, one for Group and one for Others) are converted to decimal and written as three digits. To do this remember read permission has the value 4, write permission has the value 2, and execute permission has the value 1. Add the values together to get a decimal number.

000	0
001	1
010	2
011	3
100	4
101	5
110	6
111	7

For example, read and execute permission ("101") has the value 4 + 1 = 5.

Some people prefer to use the numeric forms, especially when wanting to set a whole group of permissions together. To give all permissions to all sets of users, use this command:

```
chmod 777 filename
```

And to give full access to a file's owner user, but only read and execute permission to all others, use:

```
chmod 755 filename
```

Finally, to give read/write access to a non-executable file's owner user, but only read permission to all others, use:

```
chmod 644 filename
```

The Superuser

The superuser is a special user who has ultimate privilege on your Linux system. If you are the administrator then you are also the superuser. The superuser is also called "root". To log in as the superuser use the username "root".

Most administrative functions on the system, such as adding users and groups or editing system configuration files, require root privileges. This is because if normal users were allowed to do these things they could – intentionally or accidentally – cause havoc or damage to a system.

Most of the configuration files are owned by root as you will see in the "ls" listing:

```
$ls -l /etc/passwd
-rw-r--r-- root root 5 passwd
```

Most of the config-uration and system administration tasks in this book require you to be logged in as root. Those which do will have this "S" icon at the top of the page:

Which user to use?

If you are the administrator you might want to use "root" all the time, to make life easier. It is not recommended that you do this because of the possibility of accidentally damaging the system. Root can access anyone's files and delete or change anything, even write-protected files. One typing mistake could be a disaster! The normal way to use root is to log in as a normal user most of the time, switching to root only when you need special privileges.

You can switch to root either by logging into directly as "root", or from a logged-in session by using the "su" command. See "Who and SU" later (page 30).

Programs which must run as root

Some programs such as the "PPP daemon" have to be run as root. To allow normal users to run them you can make it "suid root":

```
chmod +s filename
```

Add set-user-id to normal permissions (will run with owner's permissions)

Adding a User Ⓢ

Why add a user when, as root, you can do anything on the system? Precisely *because* you can do anything.

It is considered bad practice to use root except when absolutely necessary because of the potential for accidental damage. Many important files on the system are owned by root and could easily be removed or changed by mistake if you are always logged in as root. It is preferable to set yourself up as an ordinary user without permission to affect these files.

The command to add a user is:

```
useradd -m username
```

The "-m" option ensures the home directory is created

This command must be run as root and will add a user and create a home directory for him/her, under the /home branch of the filesystem.

To set a password
If you want to set a password (normal on a multi-user system), log on as that user and enter:

```
passwd
```

To set the password of another user
Only root can do this. Enter the command like this to set another user's password:

```
passwd username
```

Adding Users to Groups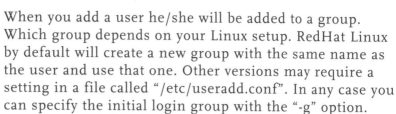

When you add a user he/she will be added to a group. Which group depends on your Linux setup. RedHat Linux by default will create a new group with the same name as the user and use that one. Other versions may require a setting in a file called "/etc/useradd.conf". In any case you can specify the initial login group with the "-g" option.

 To prevent RedHat Linux from creating a group with the same name as the user, use the "-n" switch on the useradd command.

For example, to create user "fred" and add him to group "users" issue:

```
useradd -g users fred
```

Multiple Groups

You can also specify additional groups by using the "-G" switch. To create the same user, but add him to the groups "games" and "ops" use this command:

```
useradd -g users -G games,ops fred
```

This type of thing can be useful for controlling access to certain commands or files.

Existing Users

If you want to add a user who already exists to a new group, perhaps to reflect his or her new status, you can use the usermod command to modify the user settings. This command takes the same switches as the useradd:

```
usermod -g users -G games,ops,admin fred
```

Creating Groups

To create a new group, use the "groupadd" command. The syntax is very simple, just what you would expect.

For example, to create the group "ops":

```
groupadd ops
```

Who and SU

If your Linux system has many users you might want to know who is logged on. If it is a desktop machine you may still want a list of your logged in windows. This can be done with the "who" command:

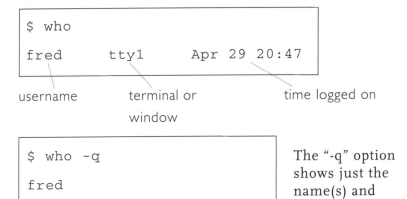

```
$ who
fred        tty1      Apr 29 20:47
```

username   terminal or   time logged on
                window

```
$ who -q
fred
#users=1
```

The "-q" option shows just the name(s) and number of users.

```
$whoami
fred
```

The "whoami" command shows your own user name.

"su" doesn't normally run the new user's login sequence and change to his/her directory. Use **"su - *user*"** to do this.

Switching User

Sometimes you want to change to another user to access some files which you don't normally have access to. Or you might want to change to root (superuser) to perform some privileged command. As long as you know the appropriate password you can do this with the "su" command:

Use "Ctrl+D" to return to the normal user.

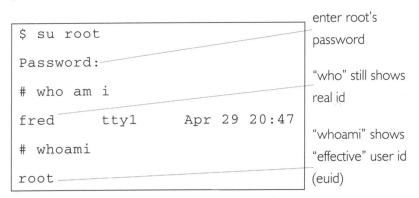

```
$ su root
Password:
# who am i
fred        tty1      Apr 29 20:47
# whoami
root
```

enter root's password

"who" still shows real id

"whoami" shows "effective" user id (euid)

Handling Disks and Files

In this chapter we will see how Linux organises files and disks. We will learn how to use different types of disks and how to get to Windows files when running Linux. We will also see how to start Linux and find out how to choose which operating system to boot up when the PC is switched on.

Covers

Chapter Three

Structure of the Filesystem

We saw before how the Linux filesystem is made up of a tree structure. You might have noticed that this structure doesn't allow for addressing individual disks like C:, D: or A: in Windows.

In Installing Linux (chapter one) we discussed how this is resolved. Each physical device, corresponding to a drive letter in DOS or Windows, is attached to the tree seamlessly as any other directory is. This process is called *Mounting* the disk.

Let's take a closer look. If you only have one hard disk partition for Linux, then you have no choice – that is where the root of the filesystem will be located. Furthermore, all the subdirectories and files in them are located on that disk too. If you have more than one partition, which is quite common these days, you have to choose one to be the root partition. Normally you will choose one to use for swap, that is for virtual memory which allows you to run more programs simultaneously. The swap partition doesn't fit into the filesystem tree. Now you can select where in your tree structure you want to place the other disks (partitions) you have for Linux. It is normal to allocate these to root-level directories according to their sizes.

All these decisions will normally be made at installation time but sometimes you want to change the arrangement, for example, if you buy a bigger hard disk.

Let's imagine we have four available partitions, each of 500 MB. This may be from a 2 GB disk split into four, for example. If they were four partitions of our second disk they would have the names hdb1, hdb2, hdb3, and hdb4. One must be root. We can use one for /home (for users to store their personal files on), one for /usr, for applications and some system files and one for /var. Here we have separated critical files and variable-sized directories which is safer.

...cont'd

The filesystem would look like this:

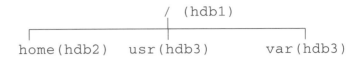

Other directories (dev, etc, tmp) would be on the same device as the root, that is hdb1. All files and subdirectories in these locations are stored on the hdb1 partition.

All files in /home and its subdirectories are stored on the hdb2 partition, and so on for /usr and /var on hdb3 and 4 respectively.

The individual disks are hidden from us. The files all appear in the filesystem in their respective directories.

How to Mount a Disk
Disks are mounted into the filesystem using the mount command. To mount a Linux-format disk on hdb2, and place it in /mnt, use this command:

```
mount -t ext2 /dev/hdb2 /mnt
```

Linux disks are called "second extended filesystem" or "ext2" type disks. The "-t" parameter determines the type or format of the disk to be mounted. Other possible values are "msdos" for a DOS format disk, "vfat" for Windows 95 or 98 and so on.

The next parameter represents the name of the partition we are mounting. All devices have a special file in the /dev directory and we specify the name of this file here, i.e. "/dev/hdb2".

The mount point is the directory in the tree where we want the disk to take root, for example, "/home". This directory must exist but should not normally contain any files. If it does they will be *covered up* by the new disk and you won't see them anyway.

The "fstab" File Ⓢ

The root partition is automatically mounted when Linux boots. However, some way is needed to mount the other disks if we are to avoid entering a sequence of "mount" commands every time we start a Linux session.

We have to tell Linux which disks to mount. The details are provided in a file called "fstab", located in the "/etc" directory.

Example fstab

```
/dev/hdb1   /       ext2    defaults  1 1

/dev/hdb2   /home  ext2    defaults  1 2

/dev/hdb3   /usr   ext2    defaults  1 2

/dev/hdb4   /var   ext2    defaults  1 2

/dev/hdb5   swap   swap    defaults  0 0

none        /proc  proc    defaults  0 0
```

The file is arranged in columns. There is a line for each partition which can be mounted. The columns are:

Device	The special file in the /dev directory for this disk or partition
Mount Point	The directory where we are going to mount it
Type	What type of disk it is
Flags	Options such as "noauto" (don't mount automatically) or "readonly" (mount for reading only)
Error Dump	Set to "1" for Linux ext2 filesystems, "0" otherwise
Check order	When to check this filesystem. "1" for root, "2" for other Linux disks, "0" for non-linux or removable disks

When the Linux system boots up, the root filesystem is automatically mounted. Then it looks through the fstab file to find out which other filesystems to mount. They can be: Linux format (ext2), other formats such as DOS or Windows, removable disks like floppy disks or CD-ROMs, or special filesystems.

All filesystems not marked with "noauto" in the flags field will be mounted. If an entry has "readonly" you will not be able to delete or change files in that directory or subdirectory.

All automatically mounted Linux disks or partitions are checked when they are mounted.

Special Filesystems

Some entries in the fstab file refer to special filesystems. One obvious is the "swap" entry. This is not even a filesystem, it is just an area of disk used by the operating system as a temporary memory store. This allows more programs to be run at the same time. Because it is not a filesystem the "swap" entry doesn't have a mount point.

The "proc" is the other special filesystem here. This is a kind of filesystem but is not located on any real disk, rather it is invented by the operating system at run-time. The mount point is "/proc" and if you look in this directory you will see many files describing the current state of the Linux system.

Accessing Windows Files ⓢ

Although Linux is a very different operating system from Windows and cannot run Windows programs (at least not without additional software), you might want to access files on your Windows disk from within Linux.

You can do this by mounting the Windows disk like any other, fitting it into the Linux filesystem's tree structure, and accessing files and folders (directories) as normal.

Windows partitions will be either FAT format, or FAT-32 format. In Linux, both are called "vfat".

If your windows disk is the first hard disk on the PC, as would normally be the case, the partition name will be "/dev/hda1".

To mount a Windows disk

1   Find out: the Linux name of the partition, the Filesystem type (vfat) and the mount point.

2   If you haven't already, create the mount point directory.

```
mkdir /windows
```

After adding a line to the fstab file, use the mount command manually to mount without rebooting.

3   Either use the mount command:

```
mount -t vfat /dev/hda1 /windows
```

4   Or add the entry to the fstab file:

```
/dev/hda1 /windows vfat defaults 0 0
```

If you used the mount command you will find your windows files in the "/windows" directory. If you left it to fstab you will have to reboot to see them.

CD-ROMs and Floppy Disks Ⓢ

CDs, floppy disks and other removable disks, must also be mounted before they can be used. However they are distinct from fixed disk partitions because you will rarely want them to be mounted automatically when you boot, as the disk will not generally be in the drive.

Always use "umount" before removing a disk, otherwise you might lose data.

To mount a removable disk we have to use the "mount" command when the disk is needed and the "umount" command when we have finished, and before it is removed.

To make things easier we can take advantage of some additional options on the fstab entry:

"user" allows normal users to mount the disk

"noauto" prevents the disk from being mounted at boot

Why do we want an entry in the fstab file if we don't want the disk to be mounted automatically? Because then we can use a much simpler version of the "mount" command.

To mount a floppy disk

1 Add this line to "/etc/fstab":

```
/dev/fd0 /floppy auto user,noauto 0 0
```

automatically determine type

allow all users to mount

don't automatically mount

2 Use this command to mount it:

```
mount /floppy
```

3 When you have finished use this command to unmount it:

```
umount /floppy
```

Because of the entry in "/etc/fstab" any user can mount the disk (not just root, the superuser) and we are able to use a much reduced form of "mount". The fstab entry fills in the missing details – the device, filesystem type, and so on.

Notice that we specified the filesystem type as "auto". This allows us to use DOS/Windows or Linux format floppy disks equally without saying which type.

This table shows different filesystem types

Disk	Device	Filesystem type
3.5" floppy	fd0,fd1	msdos,vfat,ext2
IDE CD-ROM	hdb1/2,hdc1/2, etc.	iso9660
SCSI CD-ROM	sca1/2,scb1/2, etc.	iso9660
IDE Zip, etc	hdb1/2,hdc1/2, etc.	msdos,vfat,ext2
SCSI Zip, etc	sca1/2,scb1/2	msdos,vfat,ext2

The device name for IDE and SCSI devices will depend on which position the device is in, as for IDE disks. Once you know which position it is in you can create a "soft link" to it called, for example, "/dev/cdrom", which can be used in its place in the fstab file. To link "/dev/cdrom" to "/dev/hdc1", use the following command:

```
ln -s /dev/hdc1 /dev/cdrom
```

You have to create the mount point directory if it doesn't exist.

To mount a CD-ROM

Add this line to "/etc/fstab":

```
/dev/cdrom /cdrom auto user,noauto 0 0
```

2 Use this command to mount it:

```
mount /cdrom
```

Don't forget to use "umount" when you've finished!

The "mtools" Package

Linux is usually supplied with a set of programs known as "mtools". These programs enable you to access files on DOS or Windows floppy disks without having to mount and unmount them.

The mtools programs can use the DOS-style names, i.e. "A:" or "C:". You need to use a configuration file to tell the tools which disk is which. The file is "/etc/mtools.conf" and should contain the following lines:

Add more hard disk partitions if you have them, here.

```
drive a: file="/dev/fd0" exclusive

drive b: file="/dev/fd1" exclusive


#First IDE hard disk partition

drive c: file="/dev/hda1"
```

Other mtools commands include "mcd" to change current DOS directory, "mtype" to display the contents of a file, "mren" to rename or move files, "mdel" to delete files, "mdeltree" to delete a whole directory and subdirectories, "mmd" to make a new directory, "mrd" to remove an empty directory, and "xcopy" to copy a whole directory and all its subdirectories.

When specifying filenames you can use either a drive letter defined here, or, if none is given, mtools will assume a Linux directory and filename.

To get a directory listing of a DOS or Windows disk: (you can use "-w" to display in "wide" format, or "-a" to show hidden files.

```
mdir C:\Windows
```

To copy files from a DOS or Windows disk to Linux:

```
mcopy A:\*.* /home/fred
```

CR/LF conversion

When you use "mcopy" you can omit the destination directory or filename, and it will transfer the file(s) to the current directory. One useful option in "mcopy" is "-t". This will treat the files being copied as text files and converts DOS-style line endings to Linux-style, allowing the files to be read more easily:

```
mcopy -t C:\Windows\readme.txt /usr/doc
```

Dual Booting

When you have installed Linux on a computer which already has Windows, you normally want to select to load Windows instead of Linux sometimes, perhaps to run some software which is not yet available for Linux. To do this we need a way of selecting which operating system to load when we switch on the PC.

 A partition is a disk with a letter like C: or D: in Windows.

The "active" partition is the one which has been marked as the boot partition. This partition is the one which will be used for loading the operating system. If the active partition contains Windows then Windows will be loaded; if it contains Linux, on the other hand, Linux will be started when you boot. You can change the active partition, and thereby which operating system you load, by using "fdisk" or one of the third-party applications.

It is quite inconvenient however to change the active partition each time you want to change from Linux to Windows or vice versa. Also, the frequent manipulation of the partition table is not to be encouraged generally, so there are several other ways to achieve our goal.

Loadlin
Loadlin gives us a novel way to start Linux. After starting Windows in MSDOS mode, or switching to MSDOS mode, loadlin will load Linux over the top of the currently running Windows operating system in memory (it doesn't affect the disk). Loadlin needs a Linux kernel image on the Windows disk so it takes a little extra disk space (about a half a megabyte).

LILO
Lilo is the Linux Loader and can be configured to give us a prompt at boot time in order that we can select which partition to boot from, and which operating system to load, and even which version to use. If none are selected Lilo can start a default. Lilo is normally configured during the Linux installation process but there are many ways to fine-tune it to achieve greater flexibility.

Setting Up Loadlin

Loadlin is a fairly simple procedure to set up and allows Linux to be started from a Windows session.

Your Linux disk may call the kernel a different name, e.g.. "linux", and this file and "loadlin.exe" may be in another directory, e.g. "install".

1 Create a directory called Linux on your C: drive and copy the Linux kernel and the loadlin.exe file from your Linux boot disk into it

```
C:>mkdir c:\linux

C:>copy g:\autoboot\vmlinuz c:\linux

C:>copy g:\dosutils\loadlin.exe c:\linux
```

If you are not using the original kernel from the installation disk, you could use "mcopy" to copy it from Linux to your Windows disk via a floppy disk, or even mount your Windows partition and copy it directly.

2 Create a batch file called linux.bat in the same directory

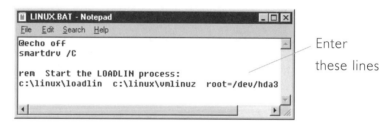

Enter these lines

3 Create a desktop shortcut to this batch file, making sure you set MSDOS mode

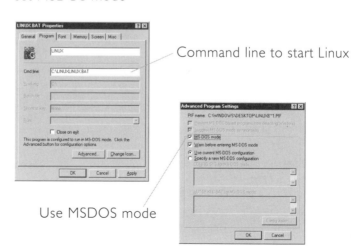

Command line to start Linux

Use MSDOS mode

LILO

Lilo must be configured from Linux, normally during the installation process. Lilo's options are held in a file called "lilo.conf", in the "/etc" directory.

Lilo configur-ation must be done by the root user.

To add a Lilo entry for a Windows partition

1 Edit */etc/lilo.conf* with "vi" or another text editor.

```
vi /etc/lilo.conf
```

Press TAß at the lilo boot prompt to see all the available options.

2 Add these lines to the file. Make sure the hard disk name and the Windows partition name are correct.

```
other=/dev/hda1
    label=Windows95
    table=/dev/hda
```

3 Save and exit the file. Then run Lilo.

```
lilo
```

To add an additional Linux Entry

1 Edit */etc/lilo.conf* with "vi" or another text editor.

```
vi /etc/lilo.conf
```

2 Add lines to show the root partition name, the location of the kernel (image) file, and a suitable label.

```
image=/boot/bzImage
    label=linux
    root=/dev/hda3
    read-only
```

Setting a timeout allows the default system to load automatically after that length of time (in tenths of seconds).

3 Save and exit the file. Then run lilo.

```
lilo
```

Other Options

You can set these other options at the top of the lilo file:

```
default=labelname
timeout=time
```

Editing and Searching files

In this chapter you will learn about "vi", the standard Unix and Linux text editor. You will learn the basic commands and how to combine them to perform more complex operations. Then you will learn about searching for strings using regular expressions, and how to use Grep to find strings in files.

Covers

Chapter Four

Basic Concepts

Although the vi editor has one of the most bizarre and seemingly non-user-friendly interfaces ever invented, it is worth learning how to use it, as it is the one editor which you can guarantee will be on every Unix or Linux system you might use.

The first, and most important, thing to learn about vi is that is has two modes: Input mode, and Command mode. When you are in input mode everything you type goes to the screen, and into the file you are editing (the only exceptions to this are cursor-movement commands and the exit from input mode command.) When you are in command mode nothing you type will go into the file you are editing; rather it will be interpreted as a command to the editor to do something. Understanding this is the key to understanding vi.

An example

1 Start vi on a new file called "testfile".

```
vi testfile
```

As usual, all commands are case-sensitive.

2 Press "i" to enter input mode. Type some text, then press *ESC*.

```
hello, this is vi|
```
cursor

3 You are back in command mode. Press "0" and the cursor will return to the beginning of the line. Press "x" 5 times and on each stroke one letter of the 1st word will be deleted.

cursor ————
```
|, this is vi
```

4 Now press ":". A colon prompt will appear on the bottom line. You are now in command entry mode. Type "q!" and press *RETURN*. This will quit vi without saving and return you to the shell prompt.

```
:q!
```

Some Useful Commands

The tables below show some useful keys to use in command mode.

Changing Mode

All the commands below go from command mode into input mode. Press ESC to change back again.

i	Insert before the character the cursor is on
a	Insert after the character the cursor is on
A	Append to the end of the line
R	Replace characters, overtyping those already there
o	Open up a new line below the current one
O	Open up a new line above the current one

Use the normal cursor movement arrows and PgUp/ PgDn keys to move between lines in the file.

Cursor movement

Use these keys in command mode.

G	Go to the last line of the file
0	Go to the first character of the line
$	Go to the end of the line

Miscellaneous Commands

J	Join current line to the next one
/abc	Find "abc", look forwards in the file
?abc	Find "abc", look backwards
n	Find next occurrence, in last direction searched
z	Undo last command
ZZ	Save file and Exit
.	Repeat last command

Colon Commands

If you press ":" (colon) a prompt will appear at the bottom of the screen. You can enter more complex commands here. Generally an exclamation mark "!" overrides a command you would not normally issue, such as quit if you have not saved the file yet. It is a way of saying "yes, I'm sure".

Getting out of Vi

:w	Write (save) file to disk
:w *filename*	Save as a new name
:w!	Save read-only file (if you have permission)
:q	Quit without saving
:q!	Quit even if you have made changes
:wq	Write file, then quit

Other colon commands

:*n*	Go to line *n*
:$	Go to last line of file
:r *filename*	Read file, insert at cursor position
:! *command*	Run a shell command
:sh	Run a temporary shell (CTRL-D returns)

Cut, Copy and Paste

Vi has some commands for removing lines, and for pasting them back in. You can also make a copy of some lines for duplication elsewhere.

Cutting out text

The command to remove a line is "dd". Generally, all Vi commands can be repeated a number of times by preceding the command with that number.

To remove 5 lines, enter

```
5dd
```

The lines removed may be discarded, or pasted in at another point in the file.

You can also delete words, with the "dw" command. Pasting (below) will paste in the word(s) removed.

Pasting commands

p	Insert line(s) below current line
P	Insert line(s) above current line

Copying lines, without removing them, is done with the "Yank" command. Press "Y" to yank one line, or nY to yank n lines. The lines pulled into the yank buffer may be inserted using paste commands as above.

Opening Multiple Files

Sometimes in Vi you want to edit two or more files, copying data from one to another. This is easy with Vi.

To copy lines between files

1 Open the first file

```
vi bigfile.txt
```

2 Copy the lines you want to paste into the other file

```
10Y
```

3 Open the other file with the ":e" command

```
:e nextfile.txt
```

4 Paste into the new file at the right place

```
p
```

5 Return to the first file, if required

```
:e#
```

Sometimes you have to edit a whole sequence of files. You don't want to enter the ":e" command for each one. Is there a quicker way? Of course there is:

1 Edit the files by putting their names individually on the command line, or entering a pattern:

```
vi *.txt
```

2 The editor starts on the first file. Edit it, then move to the next file with ":n". When you reach the last file, or at any time, you can go back to the first with ":rew" (rewind).

Mapping Keys

If you want to group together a sequence of commands for easier repetitive entry you can do that with the map command. Map allows you to define a single character, or control character to produce a complicated group of commands or a string of text when it is pressed.

 Use "h" and "l" to move the cursor left and right; and "j" and "k" to move it down and up.

Mapping to command-mode keys

The following command will:

```
:map v j0i^I^[
```

- Go down a line ("j")

- Go to beginning of the line ("o")

- Insert a tab ("i^I")

- Escape back to command mode

To insert the ESC use Ctrl+V then ESC

After entering the command, each time you press "v" in command-mode it will insert a tab at the beginning of the next line.

Mapping to "colon" commands

The map command works just as well for "colon" commands. This will map Ctrl+W to save the current file and start a new file:

- Save file

- Delete all lines in file

- Save as "untitled"

To insert the Returns use Ctrl+V then Return

```
:map ^W :w^M:1,$d^M:w untitled^M
```

 To remove a mapping use "unmap" or "unmap!". You might need to use Ctrl+V to enter the mapped keys.

Mapping in Input Mode

If you want to map a string for use in input mode, say a standard paragraph or a letter heading, use "map!".

For example:

```
:map! ^A 12 High Street,^MLondon^M
```

will insert the address when you press Ctrl+A.

Searching for Strings

There are several commands used to find strings in files you are editing:

Find Forwards

Press "/" then enter the string you want to find. The cursor will jump to the next occurrence of that string of characters. If the end of the file is reached the search "wraps around" and continues looking from the beginning of the file.

Find Backwards

To look backwards instead of forwards use "?" instead of "/". To repeat the last search made but in the opposite direction, use "F".

Find Next

After searching you just need to press "n" to find the next occurrence of the string, either forwards or backwards.

Replacing text

The replace command (actually "s" for substitute) is a "colon" command, so you have to press ":" before entering the command. It also acts on a range of lines. By default it will act on the current line. To work on more lines at once you have to enter a range, like this:

20	Line 20
20,30	Lines 20 to 30
1,$	Whole file

Examples

/this	Find next occurrence of "this"
?X	Find "X", looking backwards from cursor

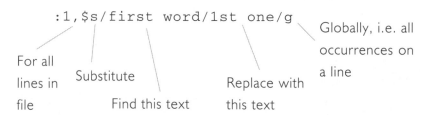

`:1,$s/first word/1st one/g`

For all lines in file   Substitute   Find this text   Replace with this text   Globally, i.e. all occurrences on a line

Regular Expressions

The search strings we have just seen are a simple example of what are called "regular expressions".

Special Characters
The following characters have special meanings:

The notation here can be used when searching for text in "vi".

`.`	Matches any single character
`c*`	Matches zero or more occurrences of character *c*
`^`	Represents the start of the line
`$`	Represents the end of the line
`[cc]`	Matches any one of the list of characters *cc*.
`[^cc]`	Any character except one of list *cc*
`\<`	Represents the start of a word
`\>`	Represents the end of a word

Lists of Characters
Inside square brackets "[" and "]" a list is formed by simply placing characters one after the other, like "[abc]". This will match "a", "b", or "c". You can indicate a range of letters with a "-", e.g. "[a-z]" will match any lower case letter.

Escaping Characters
To find a special character in the text to match, you will have to "escape" it by preceding it with a backslash ("\"). If you want to include a backslash, escape it too ("\\"). Any character which normally has a special meaning may be escaped, including "[", "]", ".", "*", "^". You do not have to do this inside square brackets, they are treated as one of the list. If you want to include "-" or "]" in a list you have to make it the first character in the list.

Examples
`[a-zA-Z]`	Any lower or uppercase letter
`^[A-Z][a-z]*`	Any upper case letter followed by optional lower case letters, at the beginning of the line.

Replacement Strings

Regular expressions are not only used for search strings, that is those you are looking for. They can also be used in the strings you specify as replacements. The following special characters can be used in "vi" in the replacement part of a substitute command:

\	Escape character (as in the search string)
&	Maps to the search string
~	Maps to the last replacement string used
\u	Uppercase letter
\l	Lowercase letter
\e	Turn off \u or \l
\L	Lowercase string
\U	Uppercase string
\E	Turn off \U or \L

Examples

`1,$s/..*/"&"/`   Enclose every non-blank line in quotes

Find one or more characters

Replace with same string, plus quotes

`1,$s/^./\u&/`   Change first letter of each line to uppercase

`s/\<[a-zA-Z][^ ]*[0-9][^ ]*/\U&\E Or \L&/g`

Start of Word

Any Letter

Anything except a space

Number

Anything except a space

Find words containing a number, replace with "*WORD* or *word.*" For example, replace "H2o" with "H2O or h2o"

Grep

One story says that "grep" takes its name from *g<regular expression>p* after the command in the "ex"editor to globally find regular expressions and print those lines. The more usual explanation is that it stands for General Regular Expression Parser. Either way, grep is one of the most useful Linux commands.

Grep, simply put, is a utility for finding strings in files. You can run it directly on a file, or files, or you can use it as a filter in a pipeline.

It is best to enclose search strings in quotes to avoid shell expansion:

```
grep "this" myfile.txt
```

Show all lines containing "this" in "myfile.txt"

```
ls -1 | grep -c "^[^A-Z]"
```

Count how many files do not begin with a capital letter

Useful Switches

-c	Only print a count of lines which match
-f	Don't show filenames, only matching lines
-l	Don't show lines, only filenames
-i	Ignore case
-n	Print line numbers
-v	Find lines which don't match
-w	Only match whole words with the expression
-x	Only match whole lines with the expression
-q	Quiet. No output, for use in shell scripts Exit status is o if any matches are found, 1 otherwise.

Extended Regular Expressions

Some commands understand a further set of special regular expression characters. These commands are "egrep" and "gawk".

Egrep

Egrep stands for extended grep and works in a similar way to grep. Grep can be used with the "-e" switch instead.

Gawk

This is the GNU/Linux version of the standard Unix tool "awk" which is a scripting language used for text file processing. See the on-line documentation for more information about gawk.

Special Characters

These characters will not work in "vi" but will work in "egrep":

+	Match one or more
?	Match zero or one
|	Means "or" as in match A or B
(and)	Used to group expressions together

Examples

Standard regular expressions use " . . *" to mean one character or more. Extended can use " . +" to mean the same thing.

Standard: [a-zA-Z] Extended: [a-z]|[A-Z]

[A-Z][a-zA-Z]* A word which *must* begin with a capital letter (Standard)

[A-Z]?[a-zA-Z]+ A word which *may* begin with a capital letter (Extended)

The X Window System

In this chapter you will find out what the X Window System is and how Linux uses it to provide a graphical user interface. You will learn how to start and stop, and configure X, and how to run some X Window programs. You will also see the integrated desktop environments available for Linux, and find out how to log directly in to the X window system instead of the text based login.

Covers

Chapter Five

About X

The X Window System is the name of the software which provides Linux with the ability to run graphical software with windows and menus and so on. Sometimes called simply "X", this is actually just a set of standards. The free implementation provided with your Linux system is called XFree86.

Clients and servers

Normally when we talk about servers we mean the faceless machine down the hall; the clients are PCs or dumb machines which access it. In X things are reversed. The X server provides the display; traditionally that was a dedicated X terminal but now that is a special program running in your Linux PC. Think of the X server as the display driver. X clients are programs which use that display for input and output; the traditional X arrangement has them on the server down the hall but in Linux they are normally also on the PC. It is possible to have multiple X servers, located on different machines if you want. This is closer to the traditional X arrangement, but it is not very common on a Linux PC.

Window Managers

The X server provides the means to display windows, buttons, menus and so on, and also the means to get input from the keyboard and mouse. In short, it provides all the input and output the clients (programs, remember!) want. However the X server doesn't define the look and feel of the windows.

The shape, colour, icon style, and behaviour are all provided by the Window Manager. This is a special X client which interacts with X and with the other clients to make the system usable. You could run X with no window manager but the windows would have no frames, no buttons to close them, nor anything not explicitly provided by the program. To start a program you would have to find a shell prompt on a text screen. This sounds odd but it allows the environment to be flexible. There are more than a dozen X window managers around which can give you the look and feel you want.

Setting Up X

The disadvantage to all this flexibility is that before you can run X you have to configure it. Normally this will be done when you install Linux. This is not always the case, however, and you may want to change things later.

www.xfree86.org is the website of the XFree86 software which provides the free X window system in Linux.

The XFree86 Configuration File

XFree86 keeps its configuration details in a file called "XF86Config" (capitalisation is important!). Unfortunately there are multiple places this file could reside, normally in the /etc directory, but possibly in various branches beneath this directory. Luckily you don't have to edit this file directly if you don't want to because there are a couple of tools you can use to help.

XConfigurator

This is the Red Hat version of xf86config, described below. Although textual, it uses colour to good effect and simulates windows and buttons. If you have this on your system it is preferable to xf86config.

If you get the mouse type wrong you won't be able to use X properly. Exit X with Ctrl+Alt+ Backspace and try again.

"xf86config"

This program is supplied with XFree86. It asks a series of questions to which the answers are usually numbers chosen from a list. It starts by asking you about your mouse. Enter the number of your mouse type and answer any supplementary questions.

Next you will be asked about your keyboard. Answer the questions about your keyboard layout.

Don't specify a high horizontal frequency unless you know it will work with your monitor. You can damage your monitor permanently!

Now the more difficult questions start. You have to specify a monitor type. Unfortunately xf86config doesn't know about makes of monitor, only frequency ranges. Some preset types are given and you should choose one of these if you can, otherwise you will need your monitor manual to find out the horizontal and vertical frequencies. If in doubt choose a low number (one of the first preset ones) and work up. You can damage your monitor if you specify too high a horizontal frequency.

After that you have to choose your graphics card type.

There is a long list of card types, if you can't find yours try to find one with the same chipset or a compatible one.

The next question asks which X server you want to use. The sensible choice here is to take the last option offered – the one recommended in the list of cards.

Now the program will offer to make a symbolic link to the X server. This is so that running "X" will always run the correct server, whichever one you chose. Only say no here if you know what you are doing and have a good reason.

When that is done you have to enter the amount of memory you have on your display card. This is usually at least 4 Megabytes (4096K) although older cards will have less. If you enter a lower amount you will not be able to get such a high resolution display.

You are prompted for the card name – this can actually be anything and it makes sense to accept the one prompted unless you used a compatible or generic one from the list. The next question is about RAMDAC, a feature of some display cards and you should normally skip this. Also say "no" to clockchip selection as most cards don't have a programmable clock chip anyway.

The program now asks if you want to probe the card – it is a good idea to say yes as it can get more information about the capabilities of the card.

That's the really technical stuff out of the way – now you have to choose resolutions and colours. There are four colour depths available:

- 8 bits-per-pixel (256 colours)

- 16 bits-per-pixel (64 thousand colours)

- 24 and 32 bits (millions of colours)

Some cards won't work with them all. You will normally choose one (how to do this, later) but now you have to select a list of resolutions available in each colour depth.

They are given in text form "800x600" means 800 pixels horizontally and 600 pixels vertically. Unless you have a really good monitor (and good eyes) you shouldn't choose greater than this if you have a 15" monitor. I recommend 1024x768 for 17" monitors and 1280x1024 for larger screens. From the menu set your chosen resolution to be the first one in the list. This is the one which will display when you start X.

Finally you will be asked if you want to write the file to the default place. Accept this. Your X server is now configured and you can try it by entering "startx". If there is a problem it will return to a text screen with some errors displayed on screen. You can try the xf86config procedure again with some different choices. Try lower resolutions or a less ambitious monitor selection.

When you are in X you can change the resolution by pressing Ctrl+Alt+numeric pad "+" and "-". If you have to exit and can't find a way out (perhaps you don't have a window manager running) press Ctrl+Alt+backspace.

Choosing the Resolution and Number of Colours

When you have a working X setup you will want to set the colour depth and resolution. You can set the resolution by making sure your chosen resolution is first in the list. You can edit XF86Config (remember where xf86config wrote it) and find the line. Make sure you choose the right one as there will be several for different display types and colour depths.

To start X at the desired number of colours (or bits-per-pixel) you need to use "startx -- -bpp 16" or similar instead of just "startx".

If you use XDM or KDM to boot directly into X you should add "-bpp 16" or similar to the end of the server line in "/etc/X11/xdm/Xservers". The line will then look like this:

```
:0 local /usr/X11R6/bin/X -bpp 16
```

Configuring X

XSetRoot
This program can be used to set up many aspects of the appearance of the X desktop.

To set the background to a solid colour
Enter "xsetroot -solid *color*"

For example

```
xsetroot -solid blue
```

To set the background "wallpaper"
The picture should be in bitmap format. Enter the following command:

"xsetroot -bitmap *filename*"

Some bitmaps are located in "/usr/X11R6/include/X11/bitmaps".

For example (enter as one line):

```
xsetroot -bitmap /usr/X11R6/include/X11/
bitmaps/escherknot
```

You can also set the background to be a uniform grey ("xsetroot -grey") or to a cross-hatch with independent X and Y spacing. Experiment with values between 1 and 16 for X and Y. ("xsetroot -mod X Y").

Setting the cursor
To set the cursor when it is outside of any windows, enter "xsetroot -cursor_name *name*"

The default is an "X" (use name "X_cursor"). Some other interesting names you can use are

arrow; box_spiral; centre_ptr; circle; coffee_cup; diamond_cross; cross; cross_reverse; dot; dotbox; draft_large; draft_small; gumby; hand1; hand2; mouse; heart; spider; and top_left_arrow.

...cont'd

 When you have found XSet and XSetRoot settings that you like put the commands in your X start-up file to make them permanent.

XSet

This program has a similar name to "xsetroot" but is concerned with setting up aspects of the X environment which are not so visible.

DPMS

If you have an "energy star" or DPMS-compliant monitor which can go into low-power modes to save energy you can use XSet to set the following times:

> xset dpms *standby suspend off*

Standby

Time in seconds to go to "standby" mode. o=disable.

Suspend

Time in seconds to go to "suspend" mode o=disable.

Off

Time in seconds to go into DPMS "off" mode. o=disable.

You might find that you can only differentiate one or two of these modes, depending on your monitor.

Example:

```
xset dpms 120 240 300
```

Mouse Settings

You can also use XSet to control mouse behaviour. The mouse pointer can be made to move at a higher speed after you have moved it by a certain number of pixels in a short time. To set the speed multiplier and the pixel threshold enter:

> xset m *acceleration threshold*

A typical setting would be:

```
xset m 4 3
```

Starting and Stopping X

When you first log in to Linux you are in a text screen. You can start the X Window system by the command:

```
startx
```

When you enter this command the X server will start up and the display will switch to a graphical display. If you normally have 6 text virtual consoles, the X screen will be virtual terminal 7 so you can switch to a text screen with Ctrl+Alt+1 and back to X with Ctrl+Alt+7.

When the X server starts it will look for a file in your home directory called ".xinitrc" (with the dot). Any commands in this file will be run. This is normally used to start a Window Manager, to run any configuration commands like keyboard mapping, or to start X clients like the clock.

If this file doesn't exist it will look for the global xinitrc (without the dot) in the "/etc/X11R6/xinit" directory and use this instead.

When a Window Manager is specified it should be the last entry in the file. This will make sure that when you exit the Window Manager, X will exit as well.

Example .xinitrc:

If you find your backspace key doesn't work properly in X, try this command.

```
xmodmap -e 'keycode 22 = BackSpace'
afterstep
```

If there is a problem starting X the screen will return to text mode and you will see the results of the X server trying to start up on your screen. Normally this will be because there is a problem with the display settings; or some other hardware like the wrong mouse type has been specified.

Stopping X

XFree86 has a hot-key combination if you can't exit normally. Pressing Ctrl+Alt+backspace will terminate X immediately and return to text mode.

Using the Mouse

Normally in X a three-button mouse is expected. If you don't have one you should specify 3-button emulation in the X configuration. When this option is enabled, pressing both left and right buttons together will act as the middle button.

The effect of the different mouse buttons depends on both the application software you are running and on the window manager you are using. However, one aspect that is universal is copying and pasting text.

How to copy text between windows

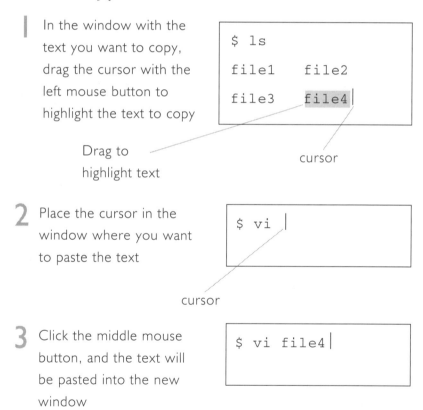

1 In the window with the text you want to copy, drag the cursor with the left mouse button to highlight the text to copy

```
$ ls
file1    file2
file3    file4|
```

Drag to highlight text

cursor

2 Place the cursor in the window where you want to paste the text

```
$ vi |
```

cursor

3 Click the middle mouse button, and the text will be pasted into the new window

```
$ vi file4|
```

Scroll Bars

Scroll bars are another important factor. In X the scroll bars, and buttons, etc. are called "widgets". They are provided not by X but by the application programs themselves. In practice however there are several standard libraries of widgets which the application programs use, such as "Athena", "Motif", "GTK", and "QT".

Most of these behave like those you see in Windows or other windowing environments but the Athena scrollbars are slightly different. These Widgets are relatively old and look their age; unfortunately this also means that they are quite widespread.

Athena Scrollbar on XTerm

scrollbar

The Athena scrollbars have a slider part, just like any others, but the slider cannot be "grabbed" with the mouse to scroll up and down. Instead, to scroll down you must click with the left mouse button anywhere along the scroll bar's length, and to scroll up click with the right mouse button.

The FVWM2 Window Manager

One of the most popular window managers in use, and the default in Red Hat Linux, is called FVWM2. This window manager can be made to behave in many ways similar to Windows, even having a similar "Start" menu.

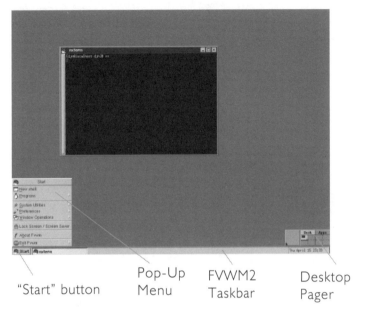

"Start" button   Pop-Up Menu   FVWM2 Taskbar   Desktop Pager

Multiple Desktops

FVWM2 as configured here has four "virtual" desktops. Windows can be dragged off the edge of the screen to the next desktop. This allows you to keep windows separate and reduce clutter. You could have a man page open on one screen, a terminal on another, and a web browser on a third.

The desktop pager shows the layout of the windows and the windows you have on them. Click on part of the pager to jump to that virtual desktop. You can also use the following keys to move around the virtual space:

Ctrl+Arrows

Jump to another desktop in the direction of the arrow.

Alt+Arrows

Move the visible part of the screen smoothly around the virtual space.

Windows

Windows can be moved around the FVWM2 desktop by clicking and dragging the menu bar with the left mouse button. You can resize a window by clicking and dragging the edge of the window. Clicking the edge with the right button shows a menu which allows you to perform the following window operations:

Restore

Restore a maximized window to default size.

Move

Move a window around the screen.

Minimize

Reduce a window to an icon, or, if you are running the FVWM2 taskbar and therefore have disabled icons, to disappear completely.

Maximize

Enlarge a window to fill the screen.

Kill

Terminate the program in the window immediately.

Close

Close the window.

The Titlebar

The titlebar can contain multiple buttons; it is usually configured to show one button at the top left which displays the window operations menu when clicked, and three on the right which perform the following: Minimize, Maximize, and Kill.

The FVWM2 Taskbar

The taskbar shows a button for each window. Clicking the button brings it to the front and restores it if it was minimized.

Focus

The window which is currently taking input is said to have the focus. This is not always the window which is currently on top. This behaviour is configurable, but the default is normally like this:

- Click on the title of a window to bring it to the top, and give it focus

- Click in the body of a window which doesn't have the focus, to give it focus (but not bring it to the top)

You can still enter text and click in windows which have the focus, even if they are not on top.

Configuration

FVWM2 is very configurable. There are way too many options to describe here. Configuration is done from a default file in "/usr/lib/X11/fvwm/.fvwm2rc", although your distribution may be set up to use "/etc/X11/fvwm2/system.fvwm2rc".

In either case it is recommended to copy this file to your home directory, and call it ".fvwm2rc". Now you can experiment with changing the settings. Settings are generally hierarchical with base styles being set, the buttons and windows are given this style with added attributes.

The basic colours are set with the following line:

DefaultColors   *WinFore WinBack TitleFore TitleBack*

For example:

```
DefaultColors Black White Yellow Blue
```

It is recommended that you read the FVWM2 man page and view any comments in the default configuration file for more information.

XTerm

XTerm is a terminal window application which allows you to enter shell commands and run text programs while you are using X. You can start XTerm with the command "xterm" or select "new shell" on the FVWM2 menu.

Start-up options

There are many command-line options which can be used with XTerm. For instance you can set the foreground and background colours with "-fg" and "-bg". To use yellow text on a blue background use this command:

```
xterm -fg yellow -bg blue
```

For other options see the xterm man page

XTerm Menus

The colours, and many other options, can be set through graphical menus once XTerm is running. There are three menus, obtained by holding the Ctrl key and clicking the Left mouse button (Main menu), the Middle mouse button (VT menu), or the Right mouse button (Font menu).

The Main menu allows you to send signals to processes, and also to secure the keyboard. When this option is selected XTerm takes control of the keyboard from the X Window system so no other process could "listen in". This may be useful for entering passwords, and so on.

The VT Menu allows you to set aspects of the terminal's configuration. Useful options on this menu include enabling the scroll bar to see text which has scrolled off the top and setting auto wrapping of long lines.

The Fonts menu allows you to set the font used in a range of sizes, ranging from "Unreadable" to "Huge"

The X File Manager

XFM is the name of a program which allows you to view and perform operations on files and directories on disks. It also allows you to start applications and is really quite powerful.

To browse the hard disk

Before running xfm for the first time, enter "xfm.install" to set up the default configuration options.

1 Start the file manager by entering "xfm"

Scroll up and down with right and left mouse buttons

File icons – Double-click to open, run, or drag to an application icon

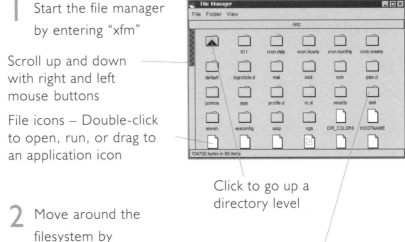

Click to go up a directory level

2 Move around the filesystem by clicking with the mouse

Folder icons – Double click to open

You can't type anything in the xfm dialog boxes unless the mouse pointer is inside the text field you are typing in.

Using the "File" menu you can: Create a new (empty file; Move or rename a file; Create a soft link to a file; Delete a file; or Make a copy of a file

In the "Folder" menu are options to: Create a new folder (directory); Go to your home directory, or up a level; Empty a directory; or Close the current xfm window.

The "View" menu has options to select how your files and folders are shown: as Icons; as Text; or as a Tree. You can also sort the display by name, date or size; Filter by name so only some files are shown; Hide folders (so you can only see files in a directory); Mix up files and folders in the display (turning this option off places all folders in the window first, before any files are shown); and you can choose whether hidden files (those whose names begin with a dot) are shown.

File Types

When you double-click a file what happens depends on the settings in the "xfmrc" file. If the file is executable it will be run, otherwise its name will be matched against entries in the config file. Each entry looks like this:

For more about file actions see the xfm application window.

pattern:icon:push action:drop action

E.g. `*.c:xfm_c.xpm:xedit $*:`

Clicking with the right mouse button on a file or folder gives a context menu which offers a choice of operations to perform on the file or folder.

Clicking on a File

The context menu for a file gives the option to edit, view, move or copy the file, create a soft link, delete the file, see file information, or change permissions.

Permissions are shown as 9 boxes – click in each one to give or take away permission.

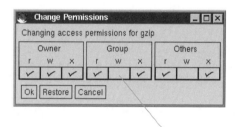

Click to set or reset permissions

Clicking on a Folder

The menu for a folder allows you to open the folder, move, copy or link, delete, see information, or set permissions.

The XFM Application Window

When starting XFM you also see a second window called the Application Window. This window contains icons which represent application programs, groups of applications, and special operations you can perform.

You can right-click the icons to delete, cut, copy, and paste them.

Icon files for use in xfm are available in this folder: **/usr/X11R6/lib/X11/pixmaps**

In the "drop action" field, use "$*" to mean the filenames dragged.

Special "action" commands include "EDIT" or "VIEW" for files, "OPEN" for directories, and "LOAD" to show another application icon file.

Click application icons to start programs

Drag file to editor icon to edit

Click group icon to open another application group

Drag files to printer to print them

Click Diskette icon to mount and open window

Drag files to trash, and Click to open

Editing or Adding Application icons

1 Right click on a blank area of the application window and choose "Install"
or Right click on an icon and choose "Edit"

2 Fill in the name here

3 Type default directory if required

4 File to pass to command

5 Name of icon file to use

6 Command when double-clicked

7 Command when file(s) dropped

Useful X Applications

There are many applications you will use in X. To start a program for which you don't have a menu item, or an icon for, run an XTerm window and enter the program's name at the shell prompt.

The X Editor

When editing text, sometimes you will use vi in an XTerm window. Other times you might want to use the X editor. Start it by entering "xedit" or "xedit *filename*".

Click to quit

Click to save current file

Click on the "Load" button after choosing the file

To open a new file, enter its name here

Editing area

Message area

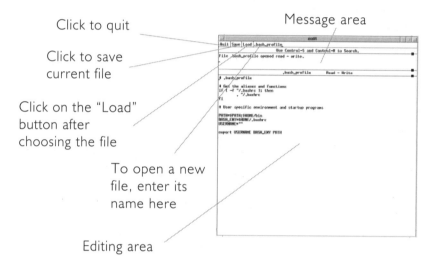

To Find or Replace text

1 Press Ctrl+S to search forwards, or Ctrl+R to search in reverse

2 Enter text to find

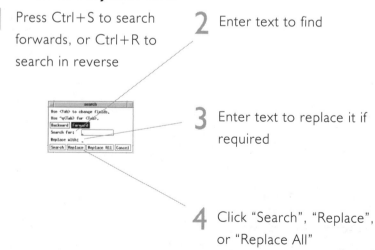

3 Enter text to replace it if required

4 Click "Search", "Replace", or "Replace All"

Xman

This is an X application for showing the on-line manual pages. (See also chapter 13). Start it with "xman" and you will see the main xman window:

Click for xman instructions

1 Click to see main page

2 Choose a manual section from the menu

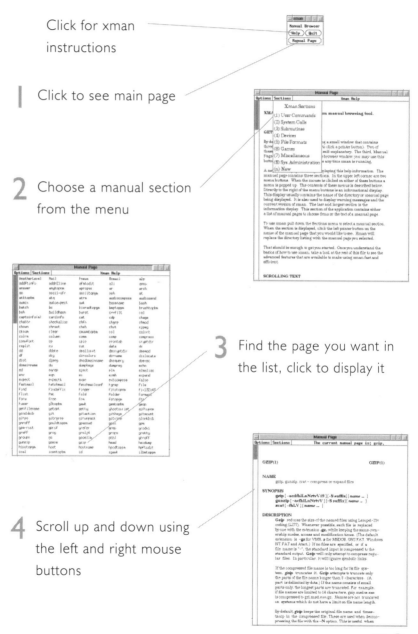

3 Find the page you want in the list, click to display it

4 Scroll up and down using the left and right mouse buttons

XClock

This simple application does what you'd expect: It displays a clock on the screen. Xclock accepts the following options on the command line:

-analog   Display a round analog clock, as shown

-digital   Display the date and time as text

-hd *colour*   Set the colour of the clock hands

-update *secs* Update every *secs*. Less than 30 gives a second hand

-chime   Clock chimes on the hour and half-hour

XCalculator

Run with "xcalc", this is a standard calculator type application. You can use the numerical keypad or click on the buttons.

XEyes

This is a novelty application which displays a pair of eyes on the screen. They follow the mouse pointer, looking wherever it goes. You can set the colours with "-fg", "-bg", "-outline", and "-center" each followed by a colour name.

System Load

XLoad

This program displays a moving graph of the current processor load. Useful if you like to see that kind of thing.

Options are:

-hl *colour*   highlight colour

-update *secs* Update every *secs*

-jumpscroll *n* How much to jump when the graph reaches the far right. Set to 1 for smooth scrolling

-label   Label to put above the graph

Standard Options

Many X applications use the same methods of displaying their windows and consequently understand the same command line options. You have seen some already, but some more are shown here:

`-geometry` *widthxheight+Xoffset+Yoffset*

Set size and position of the window. *width* and *height* are in pixels or characters, depending on the application. *Xoffset* is the number of pixels from the left edge, or the right edge if negative. *Yoffset* is the number of pixels from the top edge, or the bottom if negative. This means that the four corners of the screen are:

+0+0	Top Left	+0-0	Top Right
-0-0	Bottom Right	+0-0	Bottom Left

`-bg` *colour*

Sets the background colour

`-bd` *colour*

Sets the border colour

`-fg` *colour*

Sets the foreground colour

`-fn` *colour*

Sets the Font

`-bw` *n*

Sets the Border width

`-title` *title-string*

Sets the window title

`-xrm` *resource-setting*

Sets a resource understood by that application. See "X Resources".

X Resources

Resources are a standard X way of supplying fixed parameters to programs. A resource is a named value and can be given either on the command line or in a resources file.

Format of resources
A resource string has the following form:
*application*attribute[*attribute]:value*

The bracketed part is optional and depends on the resource you are setting.

Read the man page for a command to find out which resources it supports.

Examples

XTerm*scrollBar:on	Turns XTerm scrollbar on
XTerm*scrollBar*width:5	Set the width of the XTerm scrollbar.

Specifying Resources on the Command Line
To set a resource value on the command line of a program, use the "-xrm" option. You need to enclose the resource string in quotes as it contains asterisks which might be interpreted by the shell.

For Example
(enter as one line)

```
xterm -fg yellow -bg blue -xrm
"XTerm*scrollBar:on"
```

Specifying Resources in a File
Create a file in your home directory called ".Xresources" and place each resource string, one per line.

To make X read these resources in when it starts up you need to use the "xrdb" command. Add the following line to your X start-up file:

```
xrdb -merge $HOME/.Xresources
```

The X Screensaver

To use the X screensaver you need to install the "xscreensaver" package. The package comprises 3 main parts: the screensaver daemon (background process) which runs constantly and responds to requests; the screensaver command client, which requests that the server part does things; and the graphics "hacks", as they are called, which are the modules used for displaying different patterns when the screensaver kicks in.

To run the screensaver

1 Run the background process from your X start-up file

```
xscreensaver&
```

2 To see a demo of the screensaver modules click "demo" before the splash screen disappears

3 Click on the module name to see a demo. The command for that module is shown below

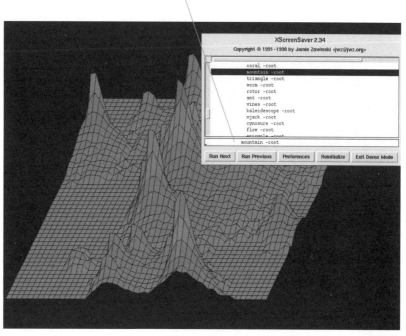

...cont'd

Setting Preferences

You can set preferences by clicking the "preferences" button on the demo window. Alternatively you can use the command program:

```
xscreensaver-command -prefs
```

Enter time before screensaver kicks in

Enter time before screensaver pattern changes

Enter time before screen locks (login password required)

Enter time before password prompt disappears

The configuration file

X screensaver is configured through a file in your home directory called ".xscreensaver". A default one will be set up when you run xscreensaver, and you can change the preferences above with lines: "timeout: n", "cycle: n", "lock: n", and "passwdTimeout: n". You can also turn screensaver fade-in with "fade", and fade-back to normal with "unfade".

In each case, n is the time in minutes.

You can set the programs used like this:

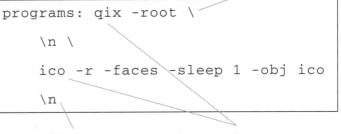

End each line with a backslash

```
programs: qix -root \
    \n \
    ico -r -faces -sleep 1 -obj ico
    \n
```

Use backslash-n for newline

Programs to run

Logging in to X directly Ⓢ

When you start Linux it enters a "runlevel". The runlevel determines what programs start. The runlevels are:

0	Halt
1	Single User
2	Multiuser, no network
3	Multiuser with network
4	Unused
5	X11
6	Reboot

These runlevels are defined in the "inittab" file, which is in the "/etc" directory.

```
id:3:initdefault:
```

There is a default runlevel, indicated by an entry in that file like this one.

Here you can see the default runlevel is 3, which means that when you start the system it will go into normal single-user mode. This runlevel does not start the X window system so you see the text login prompt.

It would be nice to see a window showing a login prompt instead. Using a program called "xdm", or "X Display Manager" we can do this. To start xdm you can change the defaults in "/etc/inittab" to start in runlevel 5.

```
id:5:initdefault:
```

To change the default, change the "3" to "5", like this.

Default runlevel

Check the number here and use it in the default line above.

Further down in "/etc/inittab" is a line showing which program will be run when you enter runlevel 5, like this:

```
x:5:respawn:/usr/X11R6/bin/xdm -nodaemon
```

Runlevel 5   XDM Command

If you have KDE you can use KDM instead of XDM. Change "/usr/X11R6/bin/xdm" in inittab to "/opt/kde/bin/kdm"

When XDM starts it uses several files to tell it what to do. These are located in "/etc/X11R6/xdm:

Xservers: Defines your X servers (displays)

XSetup_o: Starts programs before logging in

Xsession: Start up programs when X proper starts after you have successfully logged in

Normally the defaults will be adequate. These start the X console (so you can see any system messages) before logging in, and start a window manager after logging in.

To change the programs started before logging in

1 Edit
/etc/X11R6/xdm/Xsetup_0

2 Add lines for the programs you want to run

For Example:

```
xsetroot -solid blue
```

 If you are using KDM , the Xsession file receives a parameter corresponding to the session type you choose on the KDM screen. You can make Xsession load a different window manager depending on this parameter.

To change the programs started after you log in

1 Edit
/etc/X11R6/xdm/Xsession

2 Add lines for the programs you want to run

For Example:

```
xset -cursor-name top_left_arrow
```

The K Desktop Environment

Here we look at the K desktop environment, or KDE, in more detail. You will find out how to install KDE and how the desktop works. You will see how to use the KDE file manager and how to use KDE's Internet dialler. You will also learn how to configure KDE using the control centre.

Covers

Chapter Six

Integrated Desktops

There are numerous programs available to run on the X window system – window managers, utilities, applications. Unfortunately they don't generally have a consistent look and feel or the ability to work together well. This can be achieved by using an integrated suite.

There are two available: KDE and Gnome. KDE means the "K" Desktop Environment. This was the first of the free integrated desktops available for Linux and is the most mature. Gnome is said to be more technically superior but is less mature than KDE.

Using KDE

To use KDE you must obtain the QT graphics library and a number of KDE packages. The minimum packages you need to install are: KDE-Support, KDE-Libs, and KDE-Base. To be able to do much you should also install: KDE-Utils, KDE-Network, KDE-Graphics, KDE-Multimedia, KDE-Games, and KDE-Admin.

Here you can see the KDE window manager, the task bar, and desktop panel which can accept "docked" applications or buttons. Some of 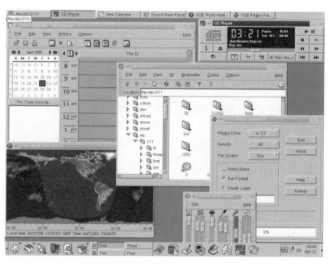 the programs are around the screen. KDE has a file manager with a tree and icon or text views. It can look into compressed files and supports web browsing and ftp. KDE also allows applications to share data by fully integrated drag & drop.

Installing KDE Ⓢ

KDE uses a 3rd-party software library called QT. QT is produced by Troll Tech and comes in two versions: a free version and a commercial version. KDE is a free software suite and so it only needs the free version of QT which is available from the KDE site as well as Troll Tech. It's also supplied with each Linux distribution which carries KDE.

To install KDE you first have to install QT. If you anticipate building any KDE packages from source you will also need the "QT-Devel" package. This will be the case if you don't have pre-built binary RPMs or TGZ packages for your distribution.

You must install "KDESupport" first, then "KDELibs", followed by "KDEBase". After that install all the other KDE packages you have. The KDE software installs by default into the "/opt/kde" directory. After installation check to see if you have a program called "usekde", located in the "/opt/kde/bin" directory. This comes with some RPM versions of KDE and makes life easier when installing.

If you are building source packages you must build and install each one before building the next one.

See chapter 9 for how to install packages.

1 Install packages using Glint or "rpm". If you have binary "tgz" packages use tar to place the files in "/opt/kde"

2 For each user, log in and run "usekde", if you have it

3 Alternatively, add these lines to "/etc/profile"

```
export KDEDIR=/opt/kde

export PATH=$KDEDIR/bin:$PATH
```

4 And edit ".xinitrc" in your home directory to contain just this one line:

```
$KDEDIR/startkde
```

The KDE Desktop

To start KDE, start X in the normal way, that is by entering "startx". This will show the KDE desktop:

HOT TIP

The KDE Help window, shown here, can show help on KDE or Linux man pages. To show a man page for "command" quickly press Alt+F2 then enter "#command".

Taskbar

Waste Bin

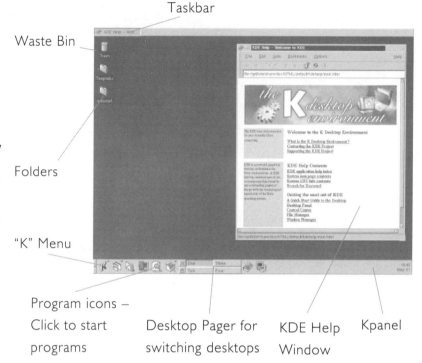

Folders

"K" Menu

Program icons – Click to start programs

Desktop Pager for switching desktops

KDE Help Window

Kpanel

The Waste Bin

Files dragged to the waste bin can be recovered later. Files deleted in the normal way (even in KDE) cannot be recovered.

The Taskbar and Kpanel

The taskbar and panel can be moved to any edge of the screen with the control panel. Here the panel is shown at the bottom of the screen and the taskbar at the top. The panel has a menu which appears when you click the "K" button. Clicking it will pop-up a menu giving access to all the KDE applications and some non-KDE ones. The panel holds buttons which can start programs with a single click. Similar icons can be placed on the desktop. These are called "kdelnk" files.

...cont'd

Creating a new Desktop Icon

1 Right-click on the desktop
   and select "New..." then
   "Program" from the menu

2 Change the name to
   something appropriate &
   click OK

3 A new icon will appear on the desktop. Right-click
   on it and choose "Properties"

4 Click the "Execute" tab

5 Enter the program to
   execute

6 You can specify a directory
   if necessary

7 Click to select an icon

8 Click on an icon and then
   click "OK"

9 Click "OK" in the main window. The
   desktop will now show the selected
   icon. Click it once to run the program

To add an icon to the panel, you must first create one on
the desktop or in a folder window (see Using KFM, page
88) then drag a copy of it to the panel.

Automatically mounting Disks

You can create an icon for a removable disk, like a CD-ROM, or a floppy disk, and it will automatically mount the disk and open a file manager window to view the disk when it is clicked.

Creating a Device Icon

1 Make sure there is an entry for the device in "/etc/fstab" (see chapter 3)

2 Right-click on the desktop and select "New.." then "File System Device"

3 Right-click the new icon and select properties, then click on the "Device" tab

4 Enter the name of the device in the "/dev" directory

KDE provides "mounted" and "unmounted" versions of icons for hard disks, floppy disks, and Zip disks.

5 Click on the icon buttons and select an icon to show when the disk is mounted, and one for when it is not mounted

6 When you click on the icon the disk will be mounted, the icon will change, and a KFM window will open to show the disk

7 To unmount the disk, right-click the icon and select "unmount"

Using KWM

KWM is the KDE window manager. Windows in KWM look like this:

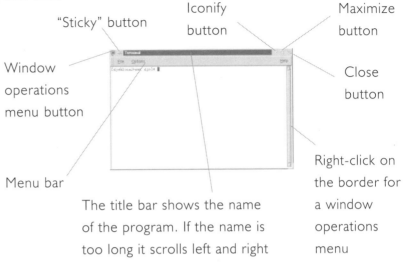

"Sticky" button

Iconify button

Maximize button

Window operations menu button

Close button

Menu bar

The title bar shows the name of the program. If the name is too long it scrolls left and right

Right-click on the border for a window operations menu

Multiple desktops

KWM provides 2, 4, or 8 desktops to work on. You can keep different windows on different desktops, and switch between desktops using Ctrl+Alt+number or using the pager on the panel. Windows can be moved from one desktop to another using the window operations menu, and marked as "sticky" so they are visible on every desktop.

You can redefine these keys using the KDE Control Centre.

KWM Keys

Alt+F1	Show "K" menu
Alt+F2	Run a program
Alt+F3	Show window operations menu
Alt+F4	Close window
Alt+Esc	(or Ctrl+Esc) Show session window
Ctrl+Alt+Esc	Kill mode. Click on a window to kill a program. ESC cancels.
Alt+Tab	Switch to next window
Ctrl+Tab	Switch to next desktop

Using KFM

KFM is the KDE file manager. To start KFM use the button on the panel, the "File manager" item on the menu, or, to start a window on a particular directory, enter

```
kfmclient folder directory
```

Up one directory level

Back to previous

Show home directory

Tree View. Click the triangles to expand or contract branches

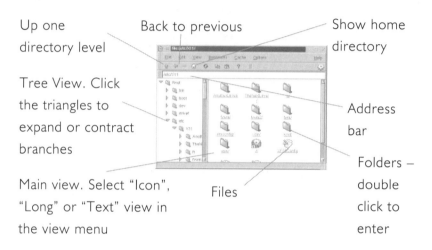

Address bar

Folders – double click to enter

Main view. Select "Icon", "Long" or "Text" view in the view menu

Files

KFM works on URLs (uniform resource locators, or internet addresses). It can be used as a file browser, a web browser, or an ftp client by entering an address of the right type in the address bar.

 If you are viewing a directory which contains a web page called "index.htm" or "index.html" KFM will display it automatically if you enable "View as web page".

For example:

```
file:///home/fred

http://www.kde.org

ftp://sunsite.unc.org/pub/linux
```

When browsing directories you can open a file by clicking on it. If KFM knows what application to use it will open automatically, otherwise it will ask you which application to use.

For FTP, you can drag files between a KFM window opened on an FTP site and a local directory. The files will be copied transparently.

Using KDE to dial the Internet

KDE has a very easy-to-use internet dialler called KPPP. To use it you will need the following information from your internet service provider (ISP):

If you don't know the type of authentication to use try PAP or CHAP.

Number to dial

Type of authentication

IP address of name server(s) and your domain name

If you have a static IP address and if so, what it is

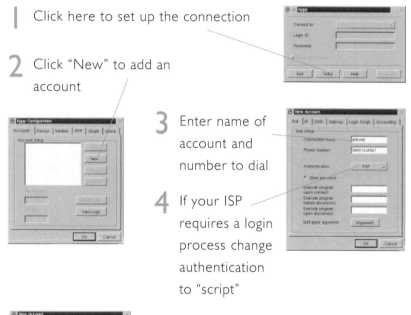

1 Click here to set up the connection

2 Click "New" to add an account

3 Enter name of account and number to dial

4 If your ISP requires a login process change authentication to "script"

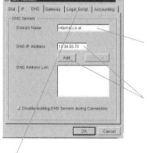

5 Enter your domain name here

6 Enter your name server address then click "Add"

7 If you chose script authentication click here and enter "expect" and "send" pairs

The KDE Control Centre

The KDE control centre allows you to configure how KDE looks and behaves. You can run the full control centre, or you can select individual sections from the menu.

Tree view of modules. Click "+" to expand tree branch. Click a module name to select it.

Currently selected module

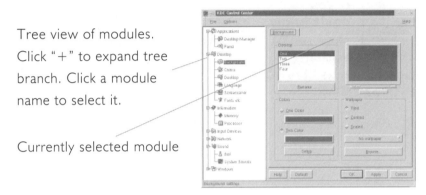

Applications
Configure the colours and settings for the file manager and web browser; also configure Panel and Taskbar settings.

Desktop
Control the appearance of the desktop, including the style and language used.

Information
Display information about your hardware devices and X.

Input Devices
Configure mouse and keyboard settings.

Keys
Change the mapping of standard KDE control keys.

Network
Control network talk utility and SAMBA networking software if it's installed.

Sound
Configure the error beep and assign sounds to events.

Windows
Change the window title bar appearance and position of the buttons. Also window behaviour and mouse actions.

KDE Applications

KEdit

This is the KDE editor. This application comes with the
KDE Utils package and allows you to do simple text file
editing that you would need for the configuration of many
Linux facilities.

Menu bar. Use to open and
save files, and to select
options such as word-wrap

Toolbar. Use for open, save,
and editing functions

Main edit window. Navigate with cursor keys and mouse. Paste
blocks of text using the KDE buttons or standard X mouse clicks.

KFind

This is more of an "applet" than an application. It is
accessed from the "K" menu on the panel and is used to
find files, either by name or by other criteria.

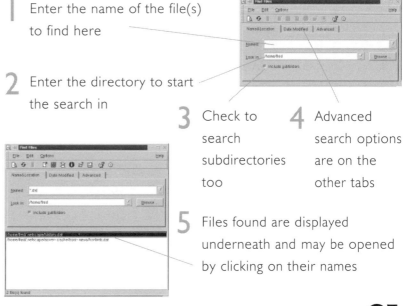

1 Enter the name of the file(s)
  to find here

2 Enter the directory to start
  the search in

3 Check to
  search
  subdirectories
  too

4 Advanced
  search options
  are on the
  other tabs

5 Files found are displayed
  underneath and may be opened
  by clicking on their names

The KDE CD Player

This application is called "KSCD" and allows you to play audio CDs through your sound card.

Note: If your "/etc/fstab" file doesn't have an entry for the CD-ROM drive you must insert one. You must also make sure that it references the real name of the device (e.g.. /dev/hdd) and not a symbolic link (like /dev/cdrom). If there is an entry for the symbolic name add one for the real name too.

Run the CD player by entering "kscd" or finding it on the "K" menu.

Play/Pause   Stop

Click to eject the CD

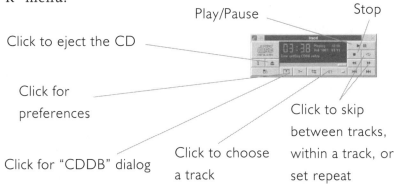

Click for
preferences

Click to skip
between tracks,
within a track, or
set repeat

Click for "CDDB" dialog

Click to choose
a track

The "CDDB" dialog allows you to enter details about a CD and its tracks in text form. The information is saved to disk so that next time you play the CD the name and artist appear, and the tracks are identified by name. It is also possible to connect to a remote database using the internet, so that if someone else has indexed this CD you will be able to benefit.

Enter name and artist of CD

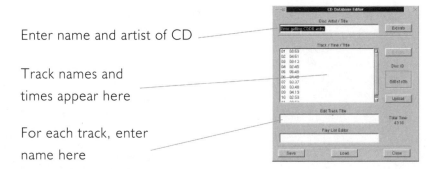

Track names and
times appear here

For each track, enter
name here

...cont'd

KOrganizer

This is a personal organizer program. You can use it to maintain a "to-do" list and one-off or recurring appointments.

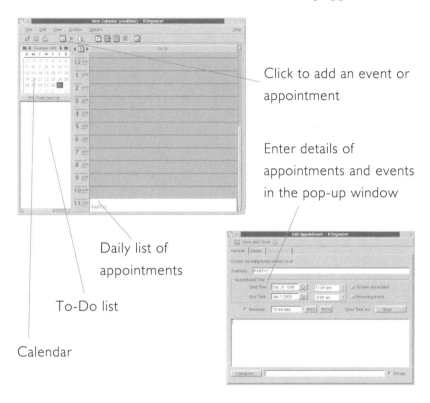

Click to add an event or appointment

Enter details of appointments and events in the pop-up window

Daily list of appointments

To-Do list

Calendar

KLyx requires the "TeX" text-processing software to be installed.

KLyx

KLyx is a wordprocessor. Unlike others you may be familiar with, KLyx makes the user concentrate on the content of the document. You can select predefined styles and KLyx will make sure your document rigidly sticks to the format. This makes it easy to produce professional looking documents.

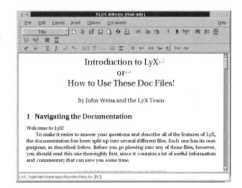

KDE Help

The KDE help browser is a multipurpose application which can show "man" pages, "info" pages, and help on all the KDE applications you have installed. There are several ways to run it. To start at the index page just enter "kdehelp".

Browser
toolbar

Web Links

KDE Application
help

"man" page
index

"Info" page
index

Search Help

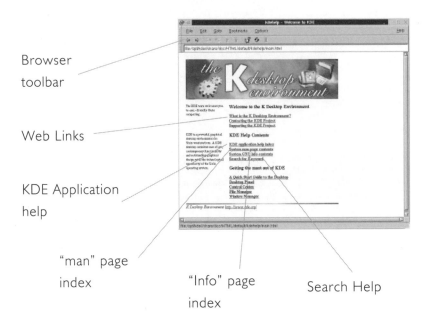

To browse help on KDE applications

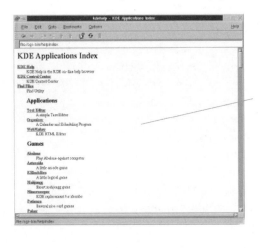

1   Click on "KDE
    Application Help"

2   Find the relevant
    page in the list
    which appears

3   The page appears in
    the window –
    browse like a web
    page

To browse system "man" pages

1 Click on "System Man Pages"

2 The list of man sections appears. Click the relevant section

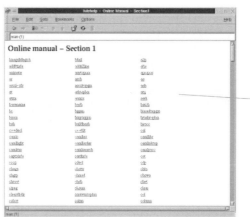

3 The index for that section appears. Click the page you want

4 The page appears in the window. You can scroll up and down or click a cross-reference to see related pages. The browsing toolbar allows you to go up a menu level

Viewing Info Pages

1   To view "Info" pages click the relevant link on the help index page

2   The directory of info pages appears. Find the one you want and click it

3   You can click on cross-references, on following pages, and on related links to browse the whole Info system

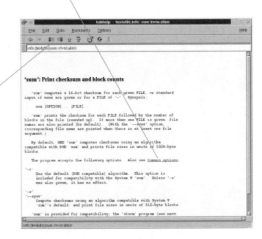

4   Click the browsing buttons to see other levels of the hierarchy and following pages in the Info topic

Connecting to the Internet

In this chapter you will learn how to connect your Linux system to the Internet and the World-Wide-Web. You will find out how to configure an autodialler, and how to start and use a web browser. Finally you will learn about using FTP to download files from remote servers.

Covers

Chapter Seven

Setting up your connection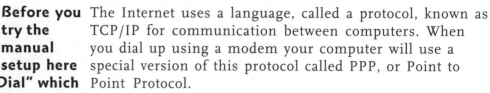

Before you try the manual setup here try "WVDial" which claims to be completely automatic, and "EZPPP" which is a graphical PPP configuration tool.

The Internet uses a language, called a protocol, known as TCP/IP for communication between computers. When you dial up using a modem your computer will use a special version of this protocol called PPP, or Point to Point Protocol.

There are several graphical tools around for configuring PPP but no clear standard as yet.

To configure PPP manually

1. You will need to find out the phone number to dial, the method of authentication, and your ISP's DNS nameserver address

Find out the details from your Internet Service Provider before you begin. If you don't know the method of authentication it is probably PAP or CHAP.

2. Copy the default PPP configuration files (your version number may vary)

```
cd  /usr/doc/ppp-2.3.5/scripts

cp  ppp-on    /etc/ppp

cp  ppp-on-dialer    /etc/ppp

cp  ppp-off   /etc/ppp
```

3. Edit /etc/ppp/ppp-on and change the values for your ISP details

```
# These are the parameters

TELEPHONE=08451234567

ACCOUNT=fred

PASSWORD=abcdefgh123

LOCAL_IP=0.0.0.0
```

1. Phone number to dial

2. Dial-up username

3. Dial-up password

4. If you have a fixed IP address put it here, otherwise zeros

5 Find the following line in /etc/ppp/ppp-on and ensure the directory path is correct:

```
DIALER_SCRIPT=/etc/ppp/ppp-on-dialer
```

 There are 3 lines shown here – each should be all on one line in the file and entered exactly as shown including the \ at the end of each line.

6 Ensure the ppp-on script points to the correct port for your modem. Change according to the table below:

```
exec /usr/sbin/pppd debug lock modem
crtscts /dev/ttys0 \

asyncmap 20A0000 escape FF kdebug 0
$LOCAL_IP:$REMOTE_IP \

noauth noipdefault netmask $NETMASK
defaultroute connect $DIALER_SCRIPT
```

COM1:	/dev/ttys0
COM2:	/dev/ttys1
COM3:	/dev/ttys2
COM4:	/dev/ttys3

Change the number according to your modem

7 Edit /etc/resolv.conf and add your ISP's nameserver address(es)

Add an extra line if you have two nameserver addresses

```
nameserver 111.222.333.444
```

The "ppp-on" script is now set up to run PPP using your modem. We still have to configure the dialler script so it can dial the number and log in to your ISP's network.

The Dial script Ⓢ

The dial script is a set of text strings with responses. The left-hand side shows what we expect to get from the modem, the right-hand side is what we send in response. You might need to change the prompts and/or responses to suit your ISP. If you don't have to enter anything in a terminal window, omit the last 2 lines (and remove the \at the end of the last remaining line). You might actually need to add one or more lines, for example to tell the remote end to go into PPP mode.

special entries

Normally you will only have to change – or remove – the last 2 lines of this script. But make sure all lines except the last one ends with a "\".

```
exec /usr/sbin/chat -v           \
  TIMEOUT            3            \
  ABORT         '\nBUSY\r'        \
  ABORT         '\nNO ANSWER\r'   \
  ABORT         '\nRINGING\r\n\r\nRINGING\r'  \
  ''        \rAT                  \
  'OK-+++\c-OK'  ATH0             \
  TIMEOUT            30           \
  OK     ATDT$TELEPHONE           \
  CONNECT            ''           \
  ogin:-ogin:      $ACCOUNT       \
  assword:     $PASSWORD
```

The login and password prompts don't have their first letter because we don't always know if they will have a capital or lower-case letter.

connected OK   login   password   sends   sends
indicator   prompt   prompt   username   password

Once this is done you can dial up by typing "/etc/ppp/ppp-on". Disconnect using /etc/ppp/ppp-off. You might have to configure PAP or CHAP first.

PAP/CHAP Ⓢ

Some ISPs use script-type authentication, where you have to respond to a login and password prompt in a terminal window. Most use a system called PAP (Password Authentication Protocol) or CHAP (Challenge Authentication Password).

Setting up PAP or CHAP

1. Edit the /etc/ppp/ppp-on-dialer file as described previously as far as the CONNECT line (with no \ on the end).

2. Edit the "/etc/ppp/ppp-on" file as before, but add the -pap user *username* or -chap user *username* to the last line, like this:

From "noauth" to the username is all one line.

```
exec /usr/sbin/pppd debug lock modem
crtscts /dev/ttyS0 \

asyncmap 20A0000 escape FF kdebug 0
$LOCAL_IP:$REMOTE_IP \

noauth noipdefault netmask $NETMASK
defaultroute connect $DIALER_SCRIPT
-pap user fred
```

using PAP authentication

Your ISP username

When this is done you can dial up to the internet by entering "/etc/ppp/ppp-on".

3. Edit "/etc/ppp/pap-secrets" (for PAP) or "/etc/ppp/chap-secrets" (for CHAP) and add the following last line:

```
username      *    password      *
```

Your ISP username

Your ISP password

Browsing the Web ⓢ

The traditional text-only web browser is called Lynx, and is still supplied with Linux distributions. However it is a little dated given that most web pages out there are intensely graphical, and Lynx is really only suitable for browsing program documentation or other text files. If you have KDE you can use KFM for WWW browsing although it is a little limited and doesn't include Java.

One of the more popular browsers in use is Netscape Navigator. It comes as part of the Communicator suite, which includes email software as we will see shortly, plus web authoring and usenet news modules.

Netscape may be supplied with your Linux distribution, otherwise you might find it on a CD given away with a magazine. Failing that you will need to download it from *ftp.netscape.com.*

I recommend using the RPM package, if your Linux distribution supports it, because it will make installation easier.

To install Netscape

1 Copy the RPM file into a suitable directory

2 Install using "rpm" or "Glint"

3 You can run Netscape by entering "netscape", or "netscape -component-bar"

Click to browse the web

Click to send or read mail

Netscape Navigator

When you start the navigator window the screen looks like this:

Navigation buttons

Click for Bookmarks Menu

Address Bar

Current web page

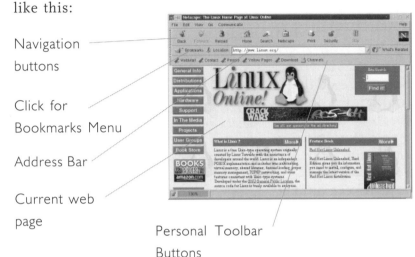

Personal Toolbar Buttons

Surfing the web

To go directly to a web page, click in the address bar and enter the URL (address) of the page. Press return to load the page. As usual you can click on highlighted links or buttons in a page to jump to other pages.

Navigation Bar

Back   Go to previous pages visited

Forward   Return if you pressed "back"

Home   Go to start page set in preferences

Bookmarks

You can store links to pages you frequently visit or which you might want to go back to, in the bookmarks menu.

To store a bookmark

1 Navigate to the page you want to store

2 Click the Bookmarks menu

3 Select "Add Bookmark" to add the link, or "File Bookmark", then a submenu to add a bookmark to that submenu

File a
bookmark
in the
"Personal
Toolbar Folder" to
make it appear as a
button on your
toolbar. If you
create a new folder
inside this folder,
and place
bookmarks in it,
you will see a menu
on the toolbar.

Managing Bookmarks

You can change, move, or delete bookmarks with the
"Manage Bookmarks" menu item. This window also
allows you to add new submenus (folders) for
bookmarks.

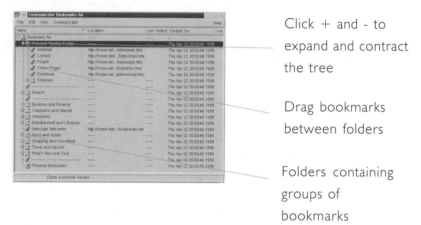

Click + and - to
expand and contract
the tree

Drag bookmarks
between folders

Folders containing
groups of
bookmarks

Proxy Servers

Some ISPs provide a web proxy server. This is a
computer on their local network where your browser can
look first to find web pages. Many popular pages are held
there and will be loaded quicker.

To configure a proxy

1 Select Preferences on
the Edit menu

2 Click here to select
proxy configuration

3 Then click the button

4 Fill in the address of the
http proxy server

5 And the port number

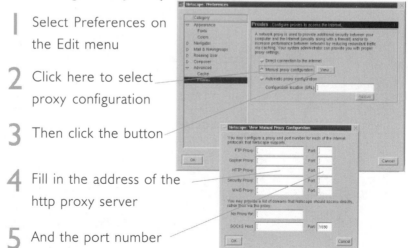

Using Netscape for Email

To use Netscape Messenger for receiving email you will need an email account with a POP3 username and password. You will need an SMTP connection for sending email.

To set up the accounts

1 Start messenger by clicking the button bar or selecting from the communicator menu

2 Choose Preferences from the Edit menu

Click on the arrow to expand mail preferences

3 Click "Identity" then fill in your details in the boxes

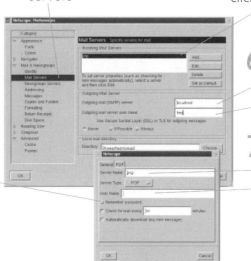

4 Click to select mail servers

5 Select POP account and click on "Edit"

Click Remember Password if you **don't want to enter your POP3 password each time you get mail.**

6 Enter SMTP server name and username here

7 Enter POP3 server name and account login name

...cont'd

Receiving and reading mail

1 Click the Get Msg button

2 Mail appears in the Inbox

3 Double-click a message to open

4 Delete unwanted messages

5 Click to show message previews

Sending Mail

1 Click New Msg, or Reply when reading a message to get the message compose window

2 Click in the box and type the recipient's address

3 Click in the subject box and type the subject of the message.

4 Enter the message here. If you are sending to someone who can accept HTML mail you can make the mail more interesting with fonts and colours

5 Click to send the message, or select Send Later on the File menu if you are not connected

Some people don't like getting HTML mail because their software can't display it. It's safer to always send plain text.

Other Mail Software

It is not necessary to use any special mail software with Linux, as it does come with a set of text-mode mail tools.

Fetchmail

Fetchmail is a utility which can check your mail on the remote server and can download any waiting messages. They are placed in the standard mail directory in your home directory and read using the "mail" program.

Configuring Fetchmail

Change the POP3 server name and the user and password for your internet account.

1 Create a file in your home directory called ".fetchmailrc", containing these lines:

2 Mail server host address

3 Protocol for mail communication (usually POP3)

```
poll pop3.demon.co.uk proto pop3
user fred
password abcdefgh123
```

4 Username for mail server

5 Put the password for the mail server here, or let fetchmail prompt you

To get mail but leave it on the server use "fetchmail --keep".

Running Fetchmail

Type "fetchmail" to get your mail. To only check messages, type "fetchmail --check".

Reading mail

Type "mail" to read mail. Pressing Return displays messages one at a time, d deletes the message. Enter q to quit from the mail program.

Sending mail with Mail and Sendmail

It is also possible to use Mail to send messages. They are actually sent by a program called "sendmail" which is normally running in the background all the time (as a daemon).

Configuring Sendmail

The first point to make is that the Mail/Sendmail combination will send mail with a From: address of your Linux login name@your Linux hostname. So make sure your Linux username is the same as your email username or people won't be able to reply properly.

Sendmail is configured with a file called "/etc/sendmail.cf". This file is quite complicated but there are really only two entries you need to set. The first is called the "Domain to Masquerade as". This means the name of your internet mail address (not including the user or @ parts). Edit this file and find a line which begins DM. It may have a comment about masquerading above it. Enter your email host and domain name:

```
DMmyhost.isp.net
```
Put your own email hostname here

Next you have to enter the name of your ISP's SMTP server. This is the computer which you send your mail to for forwarding to the recipient. (Don't confuse this with the POP3 server you get mail *from*.) It is labelled DS:

```
DSsmtp.isp.net
```
Put your own ISPs mail sending server here

Sending mail

To actually send a message, use the Mail command:

```
mail -s subject fred@somedomain.net

Hi Fred

EOT
```
press Ctrl+D to send the mail

Copying Files with FTP

Around the internet are many FTP servers which contain files for download. These files are mainly software packages but also include multimedia files such as music, images and others. FTP means File Transfer Protocol and is also used to mean the program used.

Anonymous Access

Normally you would need a password to get files from somebody else's computer. However a standard has emerged to allow anonymous access for anyone:

Username: anonymous

Password: *your email address*

Hundreds of servers the world over have agreed to anonymous access. They are often universities providing a service to the internet community, or companies providing support to customers and potential customers.

Using FTP

As usual there are graphical clients and a standard text-mode client.

Start FTP and connect to the remote site

```
ftp  sunsite.unc.edu

Connected to sunsite.unc.edu.

220-              Welcome to UNC's MetaLab ftp archives!

User: anonymous

Password:

230 Guest login ok, access restrictions apply.

ftp>
```

FTP Prompt

2 Log in with anonymous, and your email address for the password

...cont'd

3 Change to the directory you want and get a listing

```
ftp>cd /pub

ftp>ls

drwxrwsr-x 25 67    1002 1024 Apr 25 00:38
Linux

drwxr-xr-x 10 root other 512 Feb 10 22:10
UNC-info
```

Text files are "ascii" mode. Most others including programs, compressed files, and multimedia, are binary mode.

4 Choose the file type and start the download

```
ftp>binary

ftp>get  goodfile.zip
```

5 Finish the ftp session

```
ftp>bye
```

Graphical FTP Clients
Graphical FTP programs like WXFTP shown here, or KFM in the KDE suite, work in a similar way.

1 Specify address and connect

2 Navigate to the correct directory

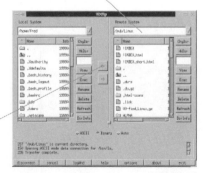

3 Initiate download by dragging or clicking

More Features

Here you will learn about setting up printing and sounds. You will see how to add a printer and how to use the Red Hat configuration tool. You will find out about printing documents and how to look at the printer queue. Then you will learn how to set up your sound card so that you can run multimedia software.

Covers

Chapter Eight

Adding a Printer Ⓢ

Printers in Linux are configured in the /etc/printcap file which describes the printers you have connected and their capabilities.

Printer Ports

Most PCs have one parallel printer port. This is known as "/dev/lp0" in Linux. If you have an older version of Linux, with a Kernel from before version 2.2.0, you should use /dev/lp1 instead.

If you have two or more printer ports, increase the number accordingly. For example; /dev/lp1, /dev/lp2 and so on.

To add a printer manually

It can be quite complex to add anything other than a text printer manually. To add support for graphics or multiple fonts, etc. use one of the printer configuration utilities (for example RedHat printtool) or read the printing HOWTO document.

1 Edit /etc/printcap and add these lines:

Don't forget the backslash (\) on the end of every line of the entry, except the last one.

printer name

port

spool directory

```
myprinter:\
        :sh:\
        :lp=/dev/lp0:\
        :sd=/var/spool/lpd/myprinter:
```

The :sh:\ line in printcap makes sure you don't get a "header" page before every printout.

2 Save the file, then add the spool directory.

```
mkdir  /var/spool/lpd/myprinter
```

Filters Ⓢ

Carriage Returns

Some printers will automatically do a carriage return when they get a line feed. Others will not. This could cause lines printed from a Linux text file to come out in steps like this:

```
line1
      line2
            line3
```

You can eliminate this problem by sending the text through a filter before printing. The filter will add a carriage return to each line feed character.

Adding the filter:

1 Create a new file in the printer's spool directory called "filter". Insert these lines exactly as shown:

```
#/bin/perl
while(<STDIN>){chop $_; print "$_\r\n";};
```

2 Add a line to /etc/printcap to use the filter:

```
myprinter:\
    :sh:\
    :lp=/dev/lp0:\
    :if=/var/spool/lpd/myprinter/filter:\
    :sd=/var/spool/lpd/myprinter:
```

PrintTool Ⓢ

More complex filters can be used to transform text and graphics into postscript or other graphic formats for your model of printer. This can be done using such software as Magicfilter – see the printing HOWTO for more information.

Filtering is usually done with Ghostscript which contains filters for many modern printer types. This is best set up with a special printer setup utility like Linuxconf or RedHat's printtool.

If you don't have a menu or an icon, you can start the RedHat control panel by entering "control-panel".

You might have to install a more recent version of GhostScript to find your printer in the list. Get this from your Linux distributor's internet site.

You can print 2,4 or even 8 pages on one sheet in reduced size if you click an option here.

Setting up a printer with Print Tool

| You can start the Print Tool by entering printtool or by clicking on this button in the RedHat control panel

2 Click to add a printer

3 Enter printer name and press Return to set spool directory

4 Click to enter printer details

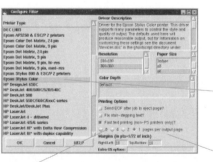

5 In the printer details window, select the printer type from the list

6 Choose required options

Printing Documents

Printing a text file can be done with the "lpr" command. This may be used as a command on its own or as a filter for other commands. E.g:

```
lp -P myprinter myfile.txt
```

To print "myfile.txt" on printer "myprinter"

```
ls -l | lp -P myprinter
```

To print the output from "ls -l"

The Default Printer

You can specify the printer to use with the -P option. Many programs, lpr included, will use a default if one is defined like this:

1 Edit your startup file, for example "$HOME/.bash_profile"

2 Add the following lines to the end:

```
PRINTER=myprinter
export PRINTER
```

Formatting text

You can use the "pr" command to format text into pages, complete with page numbers. For example, to print a listing of the "/etc" directory formatted into pages:

```
ls -l | pr | lp -P myprinter
```

Printing from applications

An application may have a printer selection window. Choose the printer from the window and click OK. It might have a place for you to enter the print command, like this:

The Print Queue

When you print a file it goes into a queue. Several files can be queued up waiting for one printer at any one time. When each job finishes the next one will be started. Separate printers have separate queues and a job on one printer doesn't have to wait for jobs on another printer to finish.

You can view the current print queue using the "lpq" command.

```
lpq -Pmyprinter ─────────┤── printer name
```

Removing items from the queue

The root user can delete all jobs for a user with "lprm -P*printer username*".

If you own an item, that is if you submitted it to the queue in the first place, you can stop items from printing. This is only possible if they haven't been printed yet. Note that modern printers have large buffers so a file could have been sent to the printer in its entirety even if nothing has come out yet.

Of course the root user can delete anybody's print jobs.

```
lprm -Pmyprinter 12345 ──── job number
```

Controlling Print Queues

The "lpc" command allows you to enable and disable printing on specific print queues. The table below shows some of the options:

lpc status *printer*	Show printer status
lpc abort *printer*	Immediately terminate printing on printer
lpc disable *printer*	Disable printing
lpc enable *printer*	Re-enable printing
lpc topq *printer job*	Move *job* to the top of the queue

Configuring Sound Ⓢ

If you have RedHat Linux you can follow the procedure here to configure your sound card. If not, your distribution may have a similar program for configuring the sound card. Otherwise follow the procedure in chapter 13 (Example: Enabling sound) to manually configure sound. If you are not using "sndconfig" go straight to the next page after you have configured your sound card.

I   Find out the I/O, IRQ, and DMA settings for your sound card. You might find them in your sound card's manual, or from the device manager in Windows.

2   Run /usr/sbin/sndconfig. The program will look for a Plug & Play sound card.

3   If your sound card is not Plug & Play you will have to choose it from the list.

4   Enter the parameters for I/O, IRQ, and DMA then tab to OK.

5   The program will test the configuration by playing a sound clip. If it didn't work check the settings entered above.

Playing Sounds

Sound Files

The Linux sound driver can play audio files directly. These have a name ending in ".au". If you have the "afterstep" window manager loaded on your system you will find some files in "/usr/share/afterstep/desktop/sounds". You might also find some in "/usr/lib/exmh*".

To test the sound driver you can send a file directly to the output device like this:

```
cat train.au >/dev/audio
```

Make sure you are in the right directory or add the directory name to the sound filename.

Controlling Volume

If you have the X window system you can control the volume of the output by using the xmixer application:

Click here to increase the volume

Click here to reduce the volume

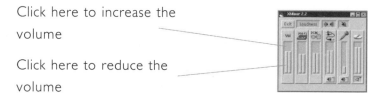

Playing CDs

You can play a CD using pcd. Make sure you have Num Lock on first, then use the numeric pad to control the CD. Use 7 to stop, and 9 to play. 8 is pause and the arrows on 4 and 6 choose tracks. Press Q to quit.

If you have X, you can also use the "xplaycd" application to play CDs. It looks like this:

Play/Stop   Pause   Random play

Volume   Repeat

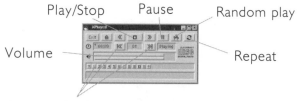

Click to choose a track

The Shell

This chapter will introduce the shell and explain the different types of shells. You will learn how to start shells and use some shell commands. You will find out what shell variables are and learn about shell programming.

Covers

Chapter Nine

What is the Shell?

A shell is a special program which gives you the familiar text mode prompt. You can use it to start other programs and it understands some special commands of its own. Sometimes these special commands are combined into a file which can be run all at once, in sequence. We call this a shell program or script.

Different shells

There are several different shell programs in use in Linux. They have many similarities but there are differences in the way they interact with the user and the commands they understand. The original shell was called the Bourne shell, or simply "sh". The program to run this is in the "/bin" directory. Current Linux distributions still have "/bin/sh" but it is often a link to another shell. The most common shell in Linux today is called Bash, which stands for Bourne Again Shell, after the popular Unix Bourne shell. Bash has more advanced features than the original Bourne shell and it is more user-friendly.

A shell very popular with programmers is called the C shell. Linux has its own version called "tcsh". This shell has more advanced shell-programming features and a different syntax for some operations.

There are other shells such as the Korn shell (ksh) and Wish or Windowing shell, which has simple graphical capabilities. Here we will concentrate on Bash as it is a popular shell and the default for most users.

Whenever you log on to a text console a shell is started automatically. In X you can start a shell by running a terminal window (such as Xterm, or Kterm in KDE). FVWM2 has a menu item to start a new shell which opens up a terminal window.

If you want to start a new or different shell you can just type its name.

For example if you are in Bash and you want to run Tcsh:

```
tcsh
```

~ means:
my home
directory.
~fred
means: Fred's home
directory.

Start-up commands
Both Bash and Tcsh will run a special script when they start up. Bash looks for a file called ".bashrc" in your home directory. This can be written using special shorthand notation as: ~/.bashrc. The C shell uses a file called ".cshrc".

When a shell starts it is normally in one of two modes: Normal, or Login Shell.

When it is acting as a login shell it will run another special shell script which usually contains commands to set up the environment, change your prompt, and so on. Your first shell in a text console will be a login shell by default and will run the special start-up script. Any subsequent shells you start will not be, unless you specifically select that with one of the commands below.

For Bash, this special login shell script is called ".bash_profile" and must also be located in your default login directory. Additionally, /etc/profile will also be run for all users by a login shell. When you exit a login shell Bash will run .bash_logout.

To start a login shell (ßash)

```
bash -login
```

Start the shell with
the -login option

For the C shell the login script is called ".login", again located in your home directory. The C shell will also execute a file called ".logout" when you exit a login shell.

To start a login C shell:

```
tcsh -l
```

Use the -l option on
its own

Shell Commands

When running commands, use single quotes (') to prevent any special characters being expanded. Double quotes (") can also be used but $ variables and back-quotes will be expanded. Back-quotes (`) containing another command cause the output of that command to be passed as arguments to the main command. Double-quotes can be used inside single quotes.

There are many commands which don't run an external program but run entirely within the shell. Some of these are used purely for controlling the operations of the shell. These commands are called shell commands.

So far you have seen how to start a program using the shell – simply type its name:

```
bash
```

A program can be run in the background, that is you get a shell prompt back immediately and cannot interact with the program, which continues to run by itself. To do this use an ampersand as the last character:

The program started and is given a process id of 123

```
cp /cdrom/* /data&
[123]
```

Redirecting Input and Output

All programs run in text mode send output to "standard output" and get input from "standard input". These are the screen and keyboard. You can redirect them so a program reads its input from another file and sends its output elsewhere.

Send output of ls command to *listing.txt*

```
ls > listing.txt
```

In Bash, you can prevent the > operator from accidentally overwriting an existing file by using the command "set -o noclobber" first.

```
banner < message.txt
```

Takes input from *message.txt* and display as a banner

Pipes

You can also send the output of one command directly to the input of another. This is done with the | (pipe) character. Several commands can be strung together e.g:

```
man ls | grep option | more
```

Shell Variables

Sometimes we want the shell to remember certain values. One of these is your home directory. The name of this directory and other values are stored in named strings called "shell variables". You can refer to the value stored in a shell variable by prefixing the name with a $ sign.

For example:

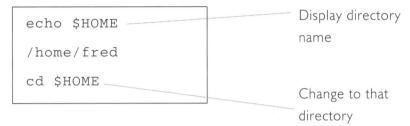

```
echo $HOME
/home/fred
cd $HOME
```

Display directory name

Change to that directory

Don't put any spaces before or after the equals sign.

If the value contains spaces put double-quotes around it "like this".

"export" is a Bash command. If you use the C shell use "setenv" instead.

To set the value of a shell variable

1 Enter *name=value:*

```
MYVAR=12345
```

Variable name

Value

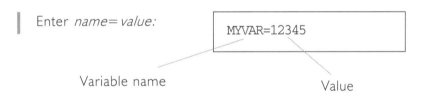

2 Export the variable to make it available to other programs:

```
export MYVAR
```

3 To see its value:

```
echo $MYVAR
12345
```

Another preset shell variable is the search path, called PATH. This holds a list of directories which the shell looks in when you type a program name.

When setting the path we normally don't want to replace what's already there, instead we want to add a new directory name to the end. We can do this by including the current value in the new string to be set:

Current value   separator   New directory name to add

```
PATH=$PATH:/etc/ppp
```

PWD is a variable which holds the current directory. That means that this command:

```
echo $PWD
```

is the same as running the "pwd"command. More useful is the OLDPWD variable. This holds the name of the directory you were in before you last did a "cd". Therefore you can quickly change back to your previous directory after perhaps checking a file in another directory. Enter:

```
cd $OLDPWD
```

Some variables which describe your terminal environment are:

COLUMNS	Holds the number of columns in your display (normally 80)
LINES	The number of lines (normally 24)
TERM	What type of terminal are you using?
SHELL	The pathname of your default shell and some which describe this instance of Bash
BASH	The pathname of the program
BASH_VERSION	What you would expect

Shell Programming

Sometimes we want to perform a complex or repetitive sequence of shell commands or programs in Linux. The easy way to do this is write a script. A script is a file containing shell commands which can interact with the user, repeat commands and make decisions.

A simple script is the "ppp-on" file we saw to start the dial-up internet connection. This script simply sets a few shell variables, then runs the "pppd" program with the appropriate options.

Let's write a slightly more complex shell script which will make backups of files to a removable zip disk. It should do the following things:

Prompt the user for the name of the directory to backup

Check the removable disk is mounted, or prompt the user to insert it

Create a backup filename incorporating the date and time

Do the backup using "tar"

To create the script, add the following commands to a file called "zipup":

```
echo "Enter Directory:"

read DIRNAME
```
Prompt user and get a string from the user using the read command.

This will only work in BASH. See later for how to use "if" in Tcsh.

```
if ! [ -d /zipdrive/lost+found ] ;
then
 echo "Insert Disk"

read A
 mount /zipdrive
fi
```
2 If the lost+found directory isn't there, the disk isn't mounted, so prompt the user and mount it.

...cont'd

To run a shell script just enter its name at the shell prompt. You might have to include the full directory path or ./ (for current directory) on the name so the shell can find it. Remember to make it executable (with chmod) before running it for the first time.

3 Make a filename using the "date" command.

```
FILENAME="bk"`date +"%U%b%Y"`.tgz
echo "Backing up to $FILENAME"
tar czvf $FILENAME $DIRNAME/*
```

4 Backup files from the directory into that filename with the "tar" command.

If...else...fi

As we saw in the backup example, we can use "if" to check for the existence of a file. There are also other conditions we can use. The general form is:

```
if [ condition ] ; then
    do something
else
    do something else
fi
```

optional "else" part if condition is not true

"if" must be finished with a "fi"

If you want to repeat a loop until a condition becomes true, instead of while it is true, you can use:

until *condition*

do

  commands

done

While loops

Sometimes we don't want to check for a condition only once, we want to continue doing something while a condition is met, or is no longer true. You can do this with a "while" loop:

```
while [ condition ] ; do
    do something
done
```

The same condition parts can be used with the "while" test as with the "if".

Conditions in Bash

The following table shows some of the conditions you can use in "if" or "while" tests:

-d *name*	*name* is a directory
-e *name*	*name* exists (file/directory)
-f *name*	*name* is a normal file
-r *name*	*name* is readable
-w *name*	*name* is writable
-x *name*	*name* is executable
string1 = string2	*string1* is equal to *string2*
string1 != string	*string1* is not equal to *string2*
number -eq *number*	numbers are equal
number -ne *number*	numbers are not equal
number1 -lt number 2	*number1* is less than *number2* (also -le less or equal)
number1 -gt number2	*number1* is greater than *number2* (also -ge greater or equal)

Negatives

By preceding the condition part with an exclamation mark (!) you can make it check for the condition being *not* true. We used this in the test for the backup shell script.

Either/Or

If you want to check for one condition or another being true you can use "-o" to mean "or". You can also use "-a" to mean "and". This is shown below:

```
if [ -r thefile -a -w thefile ] ; then

    echo "file is readable and writeable"

fi
```

"For" Loops

If you want to perform a certain action a number of times you can use a "for" loop. The "for" command cycles through a list of filenames or other words and performs commands on each one.

For example: Print each file called something.txt, and rename it with ".printed" on the end.

```
for file in *.txt do

    lpr $file

    mv $file $file.printed

done
```

The list doesn't have to be filenames. It could be words taken from another command, or the contents of a file.

For example: Copy each word from the "ls" man page to "wordlist.dat", then sort it and remove duplicates.

```
for word in `man ls` do

    echo $word >> wordlist.dat

done

sort -fd wordlist.dat | uniq
```

The C shell

In "tcsh", the Linux version of the C shell, the "for" command is replaced with the "foreach" command. The syntax is slightly different.

For example: Print all ".dat files", each preceded by "header.txt"

```
foreach file ( *.dat )

    lpr header.txt

    lpr $file

end
```

Return Codes

 To return a value from your own shell script use "exit *n*", *where* **n is the value to return.**

 It is usual for a return code of **zero to mean successful completion.**

Every program that you run in a shell returns a value to the caller. Normally you don't care what this value is but sometimes it can be useful to find out what happened when the program ran.

To view the return code from a command use the special shell variable $?, like this:

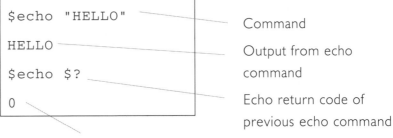

```
$echo  "HELLO"

HELLO

$echo  $?

0
```

Command

Output from echo command

Echo return code of previous echo command

Return code is 0 (success)

If the command failed for some reason the return code will be different:

```
cat xxx

cat:xxx:no such file

$echo $?

1
```

Incorrect file name

Return code shows an error occurred

Using the Return Code
The return code can be used like any other shell variable – that is, it can be written to output, or tested for success in an "if" or a loop.

 Save the return code in another **variable so you can use it more than once if necessary.**

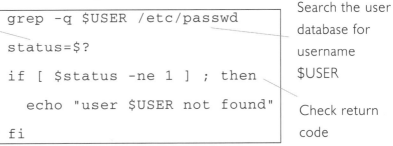

```
grep -q $USER /etc/passwd

status=$?

if [ $status -ne 1 ] ; then

   echo "user $USER not found"

fi
```

Search the user database for username $USER

Check return code

Parameters

What if you want to use a shell script, but want it to act on a different file or directory each time? Rather than change the script each time, you can use parameters so the options are specified on the command line when you call it.

As an example, let's write a simple shell script to back up all the files in a given directory, to a named tar file. We will call this "mktar.bash":

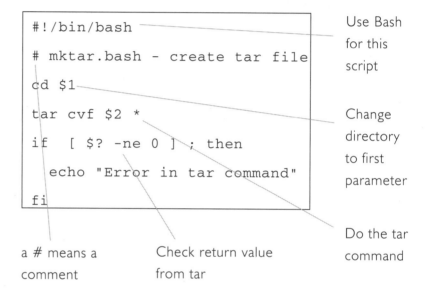

```
#!/bin/bash

# mktar.bash - create tar file

cd $1

tar cvf $2 *

if  [ $? -ne 0 ] ; then

    echo "Error in tar command"

fi
```

Use Bash for this script

Change directory to first parameter

Do the tar command

a # means a comment

Check return value from tar

To run this script just enter its name – with two parameters: a directory and a file.

For example:

```
mktar.bash mydir backup1.tar
```

As you see above parameters are numbered shell variables. The name of the script itself is $0. The real parameters start with $1, then $2, $3 and so on.

If you just want to pass all the parameters on to another program you can use "$*". You can find out how many parameters there are by checking the value of "$#". You could cycle through all parameters by using this counter, but it is easier to use a loop:

```
for p in $* do

    lpr $p

done
```

Cycle through all parameters given

Print each one

To test the value of a variable which might be empty prefix it with X on both sides, like this: This will avoid a syntax error caused by testing an empty string.

The other way to process all the arguments one by one is by using the "shift" command. This shifts all the parameters so that $2 goes into $1, $3 goes into $2, and so on. You can loop through them all like this:

```
until [ "X$1" = "X" ]
do

    lpr $1

    shift

done
```

Getopts

Some programs take formally named parameters and options, like -x or -P printer. To make processing of this type of option easier use the "getopts" command. Each time you call it, it gives you the next option and parameter, if it has one.

To use it create a shell variable containing all the possible options. Those which must take a parameter value are followed by a colon.

For example

```
OPTS="abc:"

getopts $OPTS NEXT
```

Accept -a, -b, and -c with a parameter.

Get next option and store it in $NEXT

"C" Shell Differences

If you write a script for a particular shell indicate it in the first line with a special comment which shows the path to the shell, like this: #!/bin/tcsh

Most of the examples here are for Bash, since Bash is the usual default shell in Linux. Many people like to use tcsh and some differences are presented here:

Assigning a value to a variable

In Bash you simply use *name=value*. In tcsh you have to use the "set" command:

```
set name=value
```

Additionally, to export the variable so that it is generally available, tcsh uses "setenv" instead of the Bash export:

```
setenv name value
```

Conditions

In Bash, as we have seen, conditions are in square brackets with special codes such as "-eq". In tcsh use round parentheses and double equals signs:

```
if ($STATUS==1)
```

To test other relationships you can use > (greater-than), < (less-than), >= (greater-than or equals), <= (less-than or equals), and != for not-equals. The standard Bash tests for file properties (-f, -d, -x, -w, -r) also work in tcsh.

Beginning loops

In tcsh you don't need to use "do" in a "while" or "until" loop.

Ending loops and "if" bodies

Bash uses "fi" to end an "if" and "done" to end loops. The "C" shell uses the somewhat more intuitive "endif" and simply "end" to close a loop:

```
until ($STATUS==0)
```

```
    domycommand 1 2 3

    STATUS=$?

end
```

Packages and Archives

In this chapter you will see how to create archive files and work with them. You will learn about the different ways of compressing files in Linux. You will also find out other ways of packaging software and learn how to use RPM packages. Finally you will learn what source packages are and why you might want to use them.

Covers

Chapter Ten

The Tar Command

You may already be familiar with ZIP files in Windows. Linux does have the tools to read and write these files but the most commonly used type of archive file is the "tar" file. Tar stands for "tape archive" and can be used for backing up to tape as well as creating archive files on disk. One tar file can hold many files although by default they are not compressed.

There are several graphical front-ends to tar although none of them dominates. We will look at the command-line commands here.

To create a tar archive

1 Change to the directory where the files and/or directories to be archived are

```
cd directory
```

Use an asterisk (*) to mean all files and directories.

2 Enter this command to zip up all the files and directories:

```
tar cvf myarchive.tar filenames
```

To view the contents of a tar file

```
tar tvf myarchive.tar
```

Make sure you are in the right directory when you extract files.

To extract the contents of a tar file

```
tar xvf myarchive.tar filenames
```

If you leave out the *filenames* parameter in this command, all the files in the archive will be extracted. They are extracted to the current directory and any directory names in the archive are created as it goes.

GZip Compression

The most common form of file compression used in Linux is the GZip program. GZip is normally used in one of two ways: Compressing an individual file; or compressing a tar archive.

 These commands replace the original file. To avoid this use the -c option and redirect the output to a new filename.

To compress an individual file

```
gzip myfile
```

This command *replaces* the original file. The compressed filename ends with ".gz"

To uncompress an individual file

```
gunzip myfile.gz
```

Compressed tar archives

A tar archive file can be compressed like any other file and the result will be called something like "myfile.tar.gz". It is common to get tar to do the work automatically. This is done by adding the "z" option to the tar command. These files are frequently given the shortened extension ".tgz".

To create a gzipped tar file

```
tar cvzf myarchive.tar filenames
```

To extract files from a gzipped tar file

```
tar xvzf myarchive.tar filenames
```

BZip2

There is a newer form of zip which is becoming very popular as it can have a higher compression ratio than gzip. This program is called "BZip2" and is used in a similar way to gzip or gunzip.

To compress a file

```
bzip2 myfile
```

To uncompress a file

```
bzip -u myfile.bz2
or
  bunzip2 myfile.bz2
```

There is no "bunzip2" program. To uncompress you must either use bzip2 with the -u option; or create a soft link to bzip2, called "bunzip2" and use that. The program will automatically uncompress as it is invoked as "bunzip2". To create the link enter this command (assuming that bzip2 is in the /usr/bin directory):

```
ln -s bunzip2 bzip2
```

Compressing tar archives

Some versions of tar can use bzip2 for compression. The archive file could be named something.tar.bz or something.tbz. Older versions do not directly support bzip2 but we can tell tar to use it as follows:

To create a bzipped tar file

 These commands are each entered on one line.

```
tar cvf myarchive.tar filenames
--use_compress=bzip
```

To extract files from a bzipped tar file

```
tar xvf myarchive.tar filenames
--use_compress=bunzip
```

Other Compression Programs

There are some other compression programs used in Linux although gzip is the most common.

 To exchange files with non-Linux Unix systems use compress rather than gzip and the Z option to Tar rather than z.

Compress and Uncompress

These are the traditional Unix compression tools and are still in use in many Unix systems other than Linux. Files compressed with this command have the extension .Z (capital Z).

Zip and Unzip

These are DOS/Windows PKZIP compatible zip tools although the commands are not as flexible. This type of zip file is not used very much in Linux as gzip is used in preference.

Compression Utilities

There are several utility programs you can use to work with gzipped programs. These are special versions of normal Linux programs which have been modified to automatically uncompress their input files.

zcat	Uncompress gzipped file to standard output
zcmp	Uncompress gzipped files and compare them
zdiff	Uncompress gzipped files and show differences
zgrep	Uncompress gzipped files and search for string
zmore	Display uncompressed files a screenful at a time
znew	Re-compress .Z files as .gz format

RPM Ⓢ

In addition to the "compressed tar" type of archive, there are some package formats specially designed for easy installation and management of software packages.

One of the best-known is "rpm" or RedHat Package Manager. Although invented by RedHat the program is open source and it is used by other Linux distributions too.

RPM allows you to install, upgrade and remove software packages. It tracks dependencies and will not normally allow installation of a package if it depends on another package which you don't have installed.

RPM has both a command-line interface and a graphical interface called "Glint".

 For more information about rpm use the man command.

To install a package:

```
rpm -i filename
```

To upgrade a package:

```
rpm -U filename
```

To list installed packages:

```
rpm -qa
```

To query an installed package, or a file:

```
rpm -qi packagename
or
rpm -qip filename
```

To remove (uninstall) a package:

```
rpm -e packagename
```

Glint Ⓢ

The graphical front-end to rpm is called Glint and runs in the X windows environment.

Using Glint

1. If you have an icon for Glint, click it, otherwise enter "glint" at the prompt.

```
glint
```

2. The window will show installed packages, arranged in categories. Click with the mouse to select a package.

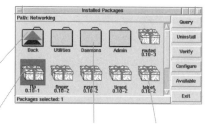

    up a level

    selected package   categories   packages
    (folders)

3. To find out about a package, select it then click "query".

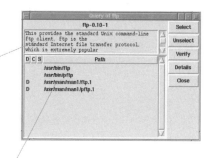

description of the package

files in the package

Software Installation with Glint Ⓢ

Glint can be used to query and install packages located on your hard disk or on a CD-ROM.

If your packages are on a CDROM, you have to mount it first.

1 Click "Configure" and enter the directory where the package files are located.

2 Click "Available" in the main Glint window.

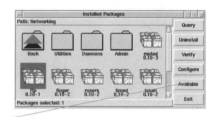

Click to see available package files

3 The window will show all packages, not yet installed, located in the directory you gave.

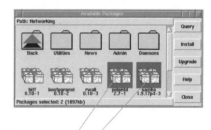

You will need to be the "root" user to install packages.

4 Select the packages you want to install and click "Query" to view information about them. Click "Install" or "Upgrade" to go ahead and install them.

DEP Packages Ⓢ

The Debian Linux distribution uses packages in its own file format called DEP. These are installed using a program called "dpkg", or the menu-driven front end called "dselect".

To install a package

```
dpkg -i filename
```

To list installed packages

```
dpkg -l name
```

optional package name to match

To remove (uninstall) a package

```
dpkg -r packagename
```

 Enter "man dpkg" for more information on dpkg, and "man dselect" for information on how to use dselect. Inside dselect press "?" to see help on using dselect and how to interpret the package display.

Using "dselect"

This is a front-end to "dpkg". Unfortunately as the man page admits, it is not very user-friendly to beginners. The basic idea is that a list of packages is maintained and when you enter "dselect" you have the following options:

Choose Access (where your package files are)

This requires you to know the "/dev" name of your CD if you are getting files from a CD-ROM.

Choose files to install/remove

You are presented with a long list of packages and their current status. You can select to install or remove them by pressing + and -. Press Q to return to the main menu.

Install or Remove chosen packages

This stage normally takes some time as it goes through the whole list of all packages in the directory.

Configure installed packages

Some packages have configuration steps which are necessary before you can run them. This is the same as running "dpkg --configure".

Source Packages Ⓢ

Sometimes a distributed software package is only suitable for your system if you have certain other packages, usually libraries, installed on your system. To avoid the problem of incompatible packages some software is distributed as "source" which then needs to be rebuilt before you can run it.

Source packages may be source RPMs, or compressed tar files.

To build a package from SRPM

1 Enter this command to build the package:

```
rpm --rebuild filename
```

You could use "glint" for step 2 instead.

2 Change to the RedHat package directory, where the newly built package is located

```
cd /usr/src/redhat/RPMS/i386
```

and install the package using the "rpm" command.

To build a package from a gzipped tar file

1 Extract the file into a temporary directory.

```
tar xvzf myarchive.tar
```

2 Read any "readme" files that the package has. If there is a "configure" script, run it.

```
./configure
```

It is best to run "make" as your own user but use "root" to install the files.

3 Run "make" to build the runnable files.

```
make
```

4 Install the runnable files.

```
make install
```

Day to Day

Here we deal with the day to day operation of a Linux system. You will learn how Linux starts up and shuts down and how to control this sequence. You will learn to protect yourself by creating a rescue boot disk, how processes run and how to manage them, managing disk space, and the operation of swap for virtual memory. You will also see some of the other commands you will come across in using your Linux system, including how to set the time.

Covers

Chapter Eleven

Shutting Down and Restarting Ⓢ

It is important that Linux is shut down properly before the power is switched off. Failing to do so could result in loss of data or corrupt disks. The correct way to shut down Linux is with the "shutdown" command.

```
/sbin/shutdown -h now
```

"shutdown" is in the "/sbin" directory

Halt the system

Shutdown right now

If you have a system with power management and software control of the power button, shutdown can turn the system off too. If the Kernel has been configured correctly the PC will turn off after halting.

Rebooting

To reboot the system you simply use -r instead of -h:

To shut down after *n* minutes from now, use "shutdown -*n*".

```
/sbin/shutdown -r 17:30 "Reboot at 17:30"
```

Reboot the system

Shutdown at 17:30

Send this message to all users

Most systems also have the following line in "/etc/inittab" which will cause the familiar "Ctrl+Alt+Del" key combination to run this command and reboot the system:

```
ca::ctrlaltdel:/sbin/shutdown -t3 -r now
```

This option gives a 3 second delay between killing the processes and restarting

Cancelling a shutdown

If you issue a command to shutdown after some time you can prevent it from shutting down by using this command:

```
/sbin/shutdown -c
```

Changing Runlevels Ⓢ

When you learned about going straight to X after booting you saw that the start-up behaviour is determined by runlevels. Recall that runlevel 3 is standard multi-user mode and runlevel 4 or 5 is multi-user with X.

When shutting down, the system goes to runlevel, 0 which is halt. Runlevel 6 means reboot the system and you will guess that "shutdown -r" goes to this level. The default is normally set to 3 or 5 and you can imagine what the consequences would be of setting it to 0 or 6 (don't try this!)

When the system is set up to auto-start in X (runlevel 5), you might sometimes want to go back to runlevel 3, with no automatic X. Why might you want this? Perhaps to try a new X start-up program or window manager.

You cannot normally exit XDM when it is started from inittab because killing the X server just restarts a new one. This is called "respawning".

You can switch runlevels with the "telinit" command, like this:

```
telinit 3
```

This command will switch the current runlevel to 3 by stopping all the relevant processes and starting all those marked for runlevel 3 (see next section). This will allow you to go to ordinary multi-user mode (runlevel 3) from another runlevel, but without rebooting. In fact you never have to reboot Linux unless you are replacing or switching kernels. Most changes can be seen by logging out and logging back in. If a background process needs to be restarted you can start it manually or by changing runlevels.

 You can also go to single-user mode by adding the word "single" after the normal boot command at the LILO prompt.

Sometimes you want to go to "single user mode" for maintenance purposes. In this mode only root can log in and a minimal set of services are started. You can do this by changing to runlevel "s".

The Init Sequence Ⓢ

Linux uses the "Sys V" init sequence. This means that it follows the start-up conventions of the famous Unix System V. These conventions determine the sequence of programs which are run when the system changes runlevels, including of course, when starting up or shutting down.

The Init Directories

Each runlevel has its own directory under "/etc/rc.d". The directories are named "rc*n*.d", where *n* is the runlevel, from 0 to 6. Each directory contains a series of shell scripts which are run in order of their names, when entering or leaving that particular runlevel. Some file names begin with "K*nn*" and are used to stop, or kill existing programs when entering that level. Others begin with "S*nn*" and they are run to start programs.

Because these files need to exist in multiple directories, one for each runlevel where the program is required, the actual scripts are located in another directory called "/etc/rc.d/init.d" and the individual runlevel directories have soft links to them.

To add a Start-up Command

To quickly add a start-up command without the complications of these scripts, you can add a command to "/etc/rc.d/rc.local" which will be run after all other scripts.

1   If a script does not exist for this program in "/etc/rc.d/init.d" then you will need to add it. It will be called with a parameter "start" or a parameter "stop".

2   cd to the directory for each runlevel where the command should be started

```
cd /etc/rc.d/rc3.d
```

3   Add a link to the start-up script and the kill script if necessary:

```
ln -s /etc/rc.d/init.d/myprog S99myprog
ln -s /etc/rc.d/init.d/myprog K99myprog
```

Making a Rescue Disk Ⓢ

 For a much more useful rescue disk, in effect a complete Linux on one floppy, you need something like "tomsrtbt" available with other bootdisks from http:// sunsite.unc.edu/ pub/Linux/system/ recovery/. Also see the "Bootdisk Howto" under your "/usr/doc" directory.

PCs and hard disks do sometimes fail and it is wise to be prepared. In the event of a failure of your PC there may come a time when you can't boot into Linux. All is not necessarily lost if you have a rescue disk which you can use to boot Linux and gain access to the system.

RedHat Rescue Disk

The RedHat installation CD has the capability to be used as a rescue disk. However, first you need to make a rescue floppy disk to use in the process:

1   Mount the RedHat installation CD and change to the "/dosutils" directory

2   Insert a blank diskette and enter this command

```
dd if=rescue.img of=/dev/fd0 bs=72k
```

3   To use the rescue disk: boot from the CD and enter "rescue" at the boot prompt. Insert the diskette when prompted

Another type of rescue disk is a simple bootable floppy containing your Linux kernel. It will help if you can't boot from your hard disk, and will start up your normal Linux system from where you can run LILO or copy a kernel for loadlin to use.

Creating a Boot Disk

You must be familiar with rebuilding the kernel for this process. See the next chapter for information on this if you are unsure.

To create a bootable kernel on a floppy disk, insert a diskette and configure the kernel as normal. When it comes to build the kernel enter "make fdImage" instead of "make bzImage".

Processes

Each program running on Linux is called a process. There are many more processes running at one time than just the programs you have started. The boot process runs a number of processes known as "daemons" for things such as looking after the print queue and networking. You can see your own processes using the "ps" command:

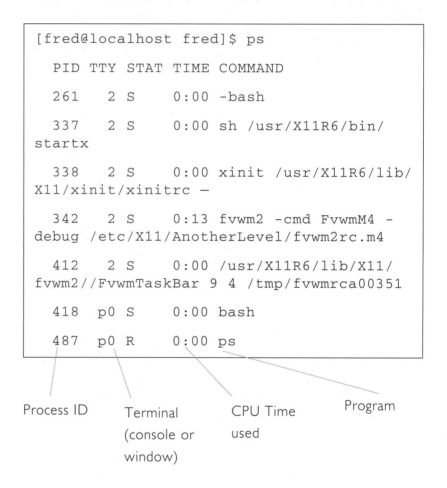

```
[fred@localhost fred]$ ps
  PID TTY STAT TIME COMMAND
  261    2 S     0:00 -bash
  337    2 S     0:00 sh /usr/X11R6/bin/
startx
  338    2 S     0:00 xinit /usr/X11R6/lib/
X11/xinit/xinitrc —
  342    2 S     0:13 fvwm2 -cmd FvwmM4 -
debug /etc/X11/AnotherLevel/fvwm2rc.m4
  412    2 S     0:00 /usr/X11R6/lib/X11/
fvwm2//FvwmTaskBar 9 4 /tmp/fvwmrca00351
  418   p0 S     0:00 bash
  487   p0 R     0:00 ps
```

Process ID   Terminal   CPU Time   Program
(console or   used
window)

This output shows the process ID and information about the programs running.

You can see all processes on the system by adding the "a" and "x" options:

```
[fred@localhost fred]$ ps ax
  PID TTY STAT TIME COMMAND
    1  ?   S     0:02 init
    2  ?   SW    0:00 (kflushd)
    3  ?   SW<   0:00 (kswapd)
    4  ?   SW    0:00 (md_thread)
    5  ?   SW    0:00 (md_thread)
   36  ?   S     0:00 /sbin/kerneld
  155  ?   S     0:00 syslogd
  164  ?   S     0:00 klogd
  186  ?   S     0:00 crond
  198  ?   S     0:00 inetd
  209  ?   S     0:00 lpd
  230  ?   S     0:00 sendmail: accepting
connections on port 25
```

Here you can see the entries for some of the system processes like the Lineprinter Daemon (lpd) and sendmail. Notice the process IDs start from 1. The process with the pid of 1 is called "init", the process which starts all others.

All processes are started by another process. That process is called the parent process, and those which it starts are called child processes. The ultimate parent of them all is "init", which you can see on the previous page. Each process has a Process ID, or pid. You can see the pid of each process in the "ps" listing. To see the pid of a process' parent use the l option. You can see the process IDs and parent IDs here (The process names are not visible because the lines are much longer):

FLAGS	UID	PID	PPID	PRI	NI	SIZE
100	500	261	1	0	0	1228

Process ID

Parent ID. You can see this process was started by the system "init" process at start-up

Stopping processes

You can send a process a signal to stop with the "kill" command. This sends the process a signal called "SIGTERM" which means "terminate". If a process is in an error condition, or if it has been programmed to "catch" SIGTERM and ignore it, or close down slowly, you can use the -9 option to kill the process immediately:

Only do this if you are sure the process you are killing has crashed, or is not responding as you could lose data.

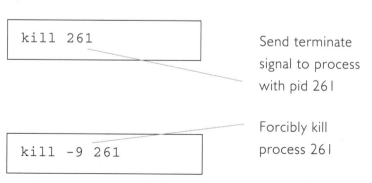

```
kill 261
```

Send terminate signal to process with pid 261

```
kill -9 261
```

Forcibly kill process 261

Monitoring Processes

Sometimes you may want to see what processes are doing, for instance if you suspect one is taking too much memory or process time. The command to do this is called "top" because it shows the top processes in terms of CPU usage.

```
 8:38pm  up 1 min,  3 users,  load average: 0.24, 0.12, 0.04

38 processes: 35 sleeping, 3 running, 0 zombie, 0 stopped

CPU states:  7.1% user,  1.7% system,  0.0% nice, 91.4% idle

Mem:   63140K av,  21920K used,  41220K free,  18452K shrd,   1156K buff

Swap:     0K av,      0K used,      0K free                 13812K cached


  PID USER     PRI  NI  SIZE  RSS SHARE STAT  LIB %CPU %MEM   TIME COMMAND

  281 root      10   0 10756  10M  1580 R       0  6.5 17.0   0:06 X

  284 fred       2   0  1268 1268   884 S       0  1.1  2.0   0:04 fvwm2

  361 fred       3   0   720  720   560 R       0  0.7  1.1   0:00 top

  357 root       1   0  1552 1552  1204 R       0  0.3  2.4   0:00 nxterm

    1 root       0   0   388  388   328 S       0  0.0  0.6   0:02 init
```

Priorities range from -19 (highest priority) to 20 (lowest priority), but users can only set positive values.

Priorities

As all the processes on the system have to share the CPU, each process has a priority, which determines how much share of the CPU it gets. You can see this on the "top" display. There is a command to affect priority of processes called "nice".

```
nice myprogram&
```

Run "myprogram" with a lower priority than usual.

Once a program is running, you can change its priority with the "renice" command. You can only affect your own processes unless you are the superuser, and you can only change the priority to a value between 0 and 20.

```
renice -2 -p 301

renice 15 -p 302
```

Reduce the priority of process id 301 by 2

Change the priority of process id 302 to 15

...cont'd

Other options to "ps"

If you want to see who is running what, use the u option to ps:

```
ps uax
```

This will show the username on the output

You can then use "grep" to see the processes for a given user:

```
ps uax | grep fred
```

This will show only fred's processes

Sorting the output

You can produce a sorted output with the "--sort" option, followed by one or more sort keys. For example:

```
ps uax --sort "uid,-size,+stime"
```

Sort by User ID | Then by memory used, in reverse order | Then in order of system time

Early versions of KTop had a bug which prevented the display from showing. If you see this, re-size the window a tiny amount with the mouse and KTop will run correctly.

KTop

If you have KDE you can use "KTop" to show the currently running processes.

Click to show processes as a "tree" showing parent-child relationships

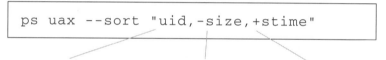

Process ID

Command running

Click to kill processes

Managing Disk Space

It is essential to monitor your disk usage to make sure you don't run out of space. The "du" command is used to show how much space you have used on disks. If you don't specify one, "du" uses the current directory as a base. It shows how much space is used in all files in the base directory and all subdirectories beneath it:

```
[fred@localhost fred]$ du /usr/src/redhat
1          /usr/src/redhat/BUILD
1          /usr/src/redhat/RPMS/i386
1          /usr/src/redhat/RPMS/noarch
3          /usr/src/redhat/RPMS
1          /usr/src/redhat/SOURCES
1          /usr/src/redhat/SPECS
1          /usr/src/redhat/SRPMS
8          /usr/src/redhat
```

Disk space used in
Kilobytes

This may produce a lot of output so it is possible to request just a summary of disk space usage:

```
$ du --summarize /usr/src/redhat
8          /usr/src/redhat
```

Total space used in
that directory and
its subdirectories

You might want to show usage in all directories but not any additional ones you have mounted. Use the "--one-file-system" option for this:

```
du --one-file-system
```

While "du" shows how much disk space has been used, it is sometimes more useful to know how much space you have left. The command to do this is "df", it stands for Disk Free:

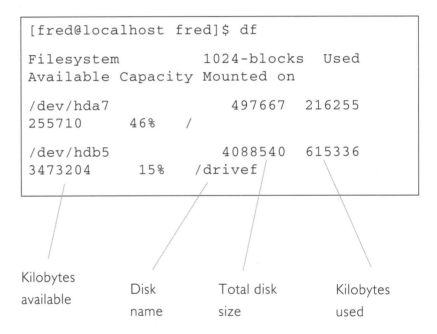

```
[fred@localhost fred]$ df
Filesystem              1024-blocks   Used
Available Capacity Mounted on
/dev/hda7                    497667   216255
255710       46%    /
/dev/hdb5                   4088540   615336
3473204      15%    /drivef
```

Kilobytes available

Disk name

Total disk size

Kilobytes used

You can give "df" a disk name to report on, otherwise it shows all mounted disks. Alternatively you can give it a directory name and it will show the disk which that directory is on. You can see above that "df" also shows the percentage of the disk which is used up.

Virtual Memory and Swap Files Ⓢ

Virtual memory is the name given to the memory which the operating system gives the impression you have. By constantly swapping "pages" from real memory to disk and back, it enables you to run many more programs or to open large data files.

The area of disk used for this is called "swap" and is usually given a partition to itself. You may have done this when you installed Linux, by specifying a partition type as "swap".

Controlling Swap
You can enable a swap device using the "swapon" command, and disable with "swapoff":

Using a swap file
You can create a special file and use that instead of a disk partition. The file should be at least the size of your RAM, unless you have more than 64 Megabytes, in which case 64M swap should be enough.

 Make sure you are the root user when entering these commands. You will need to place "/sbin" in your path too.

1 Create an empty swap file with the "dd" command (Be careful to get this command exactly right)

```
dd if=/dev/zero of=/swap bs=1024
count=32768
```

Number of blocks (this gives a 32M swapfile)   Swapfile name   Block Size=1K

2 Make swap space in this file:
```
mkswap /swap 32768
```

3 Ensure the disk is synchronised with its cache
```
sync
```

4 Enable swapping to this file
```
swapon /swap
```

Looking at Files

We have seen how to edit a file with "vi" but what about just examining the contents without the possibility of changing it? There are several ways; the simplest is to use "cat" which just writes the whole file to the screen. Unfortunately this is not always useful, especially for a large file.

Head and Tail

These two commands allow you to see just the first few lines of a file or just the end. For example, to see the top 4 lines of this "ls" command:

```
$ls -l /usr/lib | head --lines=4

total 14216

lrwxrwxrwx    1 root      root            16 Mar 21 15:48 X11 -> ../X11R6/lib/
X11

-rw-r-r-   1 root      root          1024 Sep 10  1998 cracklib_dict.hwm

-rw-r-r-   1 root      root        214266 Sep 10  1998 cracklib_dict.pwd
```

Here, "head" is being used as a filter however this is not necessary. You can use "head" and "tail" on normal files too. A very common use of "tail" is to look at the end of a system log file:

```
# tail /var/log/dmesg

FDC 0 is a National Semiconductor PC87306

md driver 0.36.3 MAX_MD_DEV=4, MAX_REAL=8

scsi : 0 hosts.

scsi : detected total.

Partition check:

 hda: hda1 hda2 < hda5 hda6 hda7 hda8 > hda3 hda4

 hdb: hdb1 hdb2 < hdb5 hdb6 hdb7 > hdb3 hdb4

hdd: 98304kB, 32/64/96 CHS, 4096 kBps, 512 sector size, 2941 rpm

hdd: no media in the drive

VFS: Mounted root (ext2 filesystem) readonly.
```

A useful feature of tail is to continuously monitor the end of an output file. Use "tail -f" (for follow) to achieve this and interrupt it with Ctrl+C.

...cont'd

 Both "more" and "less" can be used on their own with a filename, or as a filter. To use as a filter: "pipe" the output of another command with "|".

You can page through a file with the "more" command which works like "man". Press Space to go forward, b to go back, and q to quit.

"More" is quite limited and Linux has its own more advanced version called "less". "Less" understands all the commands which "more" does and others, including scrolling left and right (with the cursor control keys), and setting bookmarks and return to them. The man page for "less" shows the full set and some of the most useful are listed below:

Return	Move forward one line
y	Move back one line
Space	Move forward one page
b	Move back one page
q	Quit
/*string*	Find *string, looking forwards*
n	Find next occurrence
?*string*	Find *string*, looking backwards
N	Find next backwards
/!*string*	Find next line which doesn't contain*string*
g	Go to beginning of file
G	Go to end of file
*nn*p	Go to *nn* percent through the file
m*letter*	Mark current position with *letter*
'*letter*	Jump to mark *letter*
e *filename*	Edit new file given by *filename*
(or [or {	Find corresponding closing),], or }
) or] or }	Find corresponding opening (, [, or {

More about Disks and Files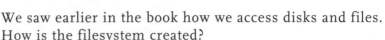

We saw earlier in the book how we access disks and files. How is the filesystem created?

Disk Formatting

Disks are formatted with the "mkfs" or "make filesystem" command. This command is a front end to several others, depending on which type of filesystem you are going to create. The syntax is:

mkfs -t *type* [*options*] *device* [*blocks*]

The options are specific to the type of filesystem being created. The standard Linux filesystem is called the 2nd extended filesystem and is denoted by "-t ext2". You can specify these options:

-c   Check for bad blocks

-l *filename*   Get list of bad blocks from *filename*

-v   Verbose output

Generally you don't need any of these options. Also, *blocks* is unnecessary as the formatter can work it out.

Example

```
mkfs -t ext2 /dev/hdb1
```

Checking a Filesystem

The "fsck" command will check the integrity of a filesystem, and repair any errors. Use it like this:

fsck [*options*] [*device*]

If the device is omitted you must specify -A option which means check all filesystems listed in the "/etc/fstab" file. If you add the -R option the root filesystem will not be checked.

You can also specify a filesystem type with "-f *type*". This will make sure only filesystems of that type are checked.

Soft and Hard Links

A link is an alternative name for an existing file. It does not make a copy of the file but it adds a directory entry, possibly in another directory or on another disk, for a file or directory.

Links can be hard or soft. A hard link must be on the same disk as the file being linked to because it is a new directory entry, indistinguishable from a real entry. Effectively the file exists twice, although the data is stored only once. If you delete a file which is hard linked, you must delete both directory entries before the file is actually deleted.

 The syntax is the opposite way round than you might expect!

Create a hard link like this:

```
ln existingname(s) newname
```

The *existingname* can be a directory or a filename, however you have to add the -d option and you must be a superuser to create a hard link to a directory. If you specify more than one the *newname* must be a directory and a link is created in it for each of the existing files or directories listed.

Creating Soft Links:

A soft link is also known as a symbolic link. The link can span across disks and is visible in "ls -l". In contrast to a hard link an ordinary user can create a link to a directory and if the existing file is removed the link remains (but doesn't work any more).

Create a soft link with the "-s" option, like this:

```
ln -s existingname(s) newname
```

Symbolic links are frequently used to give a file or directory a generic name, even though the real file or directory may change. For example:

Linking /dev/cdrom to /dev/hdd   (Special device file)

Linking /usr/X11R6/bin/X to X_svga   (X server)

The Date Command

The "date" command is used to find out the current system date and/or time. The simplest form just displays the date and time:

```
date

Fri Dec 31, 1999 12:20
```

Formatting the date and time

A useful form of the command allows you to specify the format used in the output:

Plus sign indicates format

```
date +"The time is %H:%M"

The time is 17:45
```

Special formatting characters

Some format characters are:

For the full list of formats see the man page for "date".

%a	Abbreviated Day of Week
%b	Abbreviated Month name
%m	Month 01-12
%p	AM or PM
%y	Two-digit year
%U	Day of month 01-31
%A	Day of Week full name
%B	Month full name
%H	Hour 00-23
%I	Hour 01-12
%M	Minutes 00-59
%S	Seconds 00-59
%Y	Four-digit year
%W	Week number 00-53

There are some other options you can put in the format string which you can use to affect the look of the final output.

%%	Percent sign
%n	Newline
%t	Tab character
-	Don't pad with zeroes
_	Pad with spaces instead of zeros

The formatted output version of the date command can be useful to get the date or time into another command, for example to assign a variable for later use:

```
DATE_AND_TIME=`date +"%U%m%Y %H:%M:%S"`

echo $DATE_AND_TIME

31121999 12:20:45
```

Back-quotes to get the output of the date command into the shell variable

Setting the time and date
The date command can also be used to set the time. The command is:

date -s MMddhhmmyy[.ss]

For example, to set the date and time to 09:00 on 31 December 1999:

```
date -s 1231090099
```

The Hardware Clock

Linux keeps a record of the current date and time internally, in memory. This time is set from the hardware clock when the PC is booted. When you set the time or date using the "date --set" command it is this internal time which is set. If you want to set the hardware clock, also known as the CMOS clock, you have to use a different command.

```
setclock
```
Sets hardware clock to match the current system time

You can see the state of the CMOS clock with the "clock" command. This command can also be used to set the system clock so that it is the same as the hardware clock, in effect to re-read the time from the hardware:

```
clock -a
```
Sets system clock to match the current CMOS hardware clock

Timezones

If you tell the system which timezone you are in and set the clock to GMT, the system will adjust your time correctly and allow for daylight-saving such as summer time. The list of possible timezones are in a file called "/usr/share/zoneinfo/zone.tab". There are special files corresponding to each timezone in the same directory and subdirectories.

The current timezone is set by a symbolic link called "/etc/localtime" linked to one of these special files.

Setting the Timezone

On RedHat Linux there is a program to do this. It is called "timeconfig" and you can run it with "/sbin/timeconfig". On other systems you may have to make the link yourself, for example:

This command is entered on one line.

```
ln -s /usr/share/zoneinfo/Europe/London /
etc/localtime
```

Scheduling Jobs

The Linux job scheduler is called Cron. This chapter gives an introduction to Cron and shows you how to configure jobs to run at times in the future. You will see how to set up system jobs and jobs for individual users.

Covers

Chapter Twelve

Cron

You can schedule any program, or combination of programs, to run at any time of the day or night on any date, or at regular intervals, using the Linux scheduler, "Cron".

Cron is a program which always runs in the background (as a "daemon") and the details of jobs which have been scheduled to run are kept in a file called "crontab".

There are in fact two kinds of crontab files: the system crontab and user crontabs.

The System Crontab

The system file is maintained by "root". It is edited directly using a text editor such as "vi". This file is used for scheduled system operations, for example:

- System backups

- Removing old log files

- System status reporting

- Updating system files or databases

User Crontabs

User files are not maintained by "root", but by individual users. In contrast to the system crontab file they must be maintained using a special user command to get access to the file. This command is also called "crontab".

User crontabs are used for users' own scheduled jobs. For example:

- Application reports

- Running long jobs out of hours

- Personal backups or file copying

The System Crontab Ⓢ

The system crontab file is located in "/etc/crontab". Each entry contains five date and time fields which specify when to run the job.

An entry looks like this:

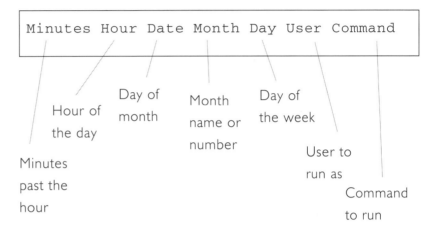

```
Minutes  Hour  Date  Month  Day  User  Command
```

Minutes past the hour

Hour of the day

Day of month

Month name or number

Day of the week

User to run as

Command to run

Each field can contain a "*" which means "all" or "any". A command will be run if the hours and minutes match, the month matches, and either the day of the month, or the day of the week matches.

Examples

1. Every day at 01:00am, remove all files more than 2 days old from /tmp:

```
00 01 * * * root find /tmp -mtime -2 -exec rm {} \;
```

2. Every monday at 8:30, create a new login message:

```
30 08 * * mon root cookie > /etc/motd
```

3. Send a message to all logged in users after midnight on Jan 1st:

```
01 00 01 jan * root echo Happy new year | wall
```

User Crontabs

The user crontab follows a similar format as the system one, but doesn't have the "user" field as all commands are run as the owning user. Each entry looks like this:

```
Minutes Hour Date Month Day Command
```

Again, each field can contain "*" to mean "all" or "any".

Creating a User Crontab

Each user has their own crontab file so if you have never set one up it won't yet exist. To create it enter this command:

```
crontab -e
```

This command will start the "vi" editor, or another if you export the EDITOR shell variable with the name of your preferred editor.

You can insert lines in the format described above. Once you have finished save and exit the editor and your file will be stored away for cron to read and act upon.

Viewing Your Crontab File

If you enter this command:

```
crontab -l
```

You will see your crontab file listed out to the screen.

To Change or Add & Remove Entries

Use the same command as when you created the file:

```
crontab -e
```

Make the necessary changes, save and exit the editor and cron will re-read the file.

More about Crontabs

Output from Cron jobs

Normally when a cron job runs the output is sent via the Linux "mail" command to the user who owns the job.

You can send the output to a file by redirecting the output, like any other command:

```
00 12 * * * root (date;df) >>/etc/cron.out
```

Alternatively you can use the cron shell variable, "MAILTO".

Cron Shell Variables

Certain special variables are active in the crontab file:

USER

The user to run the command as (not changeable).

HOME

The user's home directory.

SHELL

The shell to use to run the command.

MAILTO

Mail program to use. You can set it to "" to prevent mail being sent at all.

To set a crontab shell variable just use this form:

variable-name=value

For example:

```
SHELL=tcsh
```

Organising the System Crontab Ⓢ

Most Linux Distributions come with crontab pre-configured with certain jobs already set up. Examples are:

- Delete files from /tmp

- Manage system log files

- Update the "locate" database

In order to manage the various jobs some distributions divide them into categories such as "daily", "weekly" and "monthly", with each category having its own directory under "/etc", for example:

```
/etc/cron.daily

/etc/cron.weekly

/etc/cron.monthly
```

The actual entry in the system crontab for each interval makes a call to a shell script called "run-parts". This script will run each script or program found in the appropriate directory. For example the daily entry in "/etc/crontab" looks like this:

```
01 01 * * * root run-parts /etc/cron.daily
```

And in the directory "/etc/cron.daily" are the following scripts:

```
updatedb.cron

logrotate

tmpwatch
```

You can add other scripts here to be run once per day.

The "run-parts" script simply uses a "for" loop to cycle through all files in the directory given as a parameter and executes each one.

Kernel Configuration

The kernel contains all the drivers for various hardware devices. This chapter will show you how to configure the kernel and compile changes into it. You will learn how to run the different kernel configuration programs, how to install a new kernel and how to upgrade to the latest version of the kernel.

Covers

Chapter Thirteen

Why Reconfigure the Kernel?

The Linux Kernel is the part of the operating system which provides the "glue" between the PC's hardware and user programs, including your shell. There are many options for different types of hardware and it doesn't make sense for them all to be contained within the kernel as it would waste a lot of memory and disk space.

Instead, a typical distribution kernel will have built-in support for many of the most common hardware devices. You can tailor this to your specific needs.

Other reasons for rebuilding the kernel are; to enhance performance by fine-tuning, or to upgrade to a new version.

Kernel options can be compiled into the kernel – this means the relevant software is permanently in the memory. They can also be compiled as modules, which means that the software driver is loaded only when needed. This allows some memory to be saved and reduces the size of the kernel on disk. It is sensible to configure as many options as possible as modules, except for those which are needed at boot time or for which it would be inefficient.

Required packages

Before you start to reconfigure the kernel you must make sure you have the development tools installed. You need the GNU C compiler and development tools and the standard libraries. Additionally you will need the kernel sources. The full list you need is:

kernel-headers In "Glint" you will find this in the "Base/Kernel" group.

kernel-source   Also in the "Base/Kernel group"

gcc   In the "Development/Languages" group

glibc-devel   In "Development/Libraries"

bin86   In "Development/Languages"

make   In "Development/Building"

Config and Menuconfig Ⓢ

You can configure the kernel with one of three commands. You need to answer a series of questions or set the modules and options you would like to configure into the kernel. The most basic is with the command "make config".

```
# make config
rm -f include/asm
( cd include ; ln -sf asm-i386 asm)
/bin/sh scripts/Configure arch/i386/config.in
#
# Using defaults found in .config
#
*
* Code maturity level options
*
Prompt for development and/or incomplete code/drivers (CONFIG_EXPERIMENTAL)
[N/y/?] n
*
* Processor type and features
*
Processor family (386, 486/Cx486, 586/K5/5x86/6x86, Pentium/K6/TSC, PPro/
6x86MX) [PPro/6x86MX] 6x86
```

Answer all the questions

Enter "?" for help

To use "menuconfig" you must make sure you have the "ncurses-devel" package installed. In "Glint" this can be found under the "Development/libraries" section.

A much nicer way is to use "make menuconfig", which provides text-based windows and menus. It is shown here in a terminal window in X, but it can just as easily be run from a text console:

Choose a section by scrolling up and down with the cursor keys.

Move between fields with the Tab key, and select by pressing Enter.

In each section, select an item to include it in the Kernel.

In some items you must enter values.

Using Xconfig Ⓢ

If you have "X" the best way to configure the kernel is to use "make xconfig". This will give you a fully graphical menu system for selecting the options you want to include in the Kernel. When you enter the command (in X) you will see the following on your terminal screen:

```
[root@gnasher /root]# cd /usr/src/linux
[root@gnasher linux]# make xconfig
rm -f include/asm
( cd include ; ln -sf asm-i386 asm)
make -C scripts kconfig.tk
make[1]: Entering directory '/usr/src/linux-2.2.2/scripts'
gcc -Wall -Wstrict-prototypes -O2 -fomit-frame-pointer -c -o tkparse.o
tkparse.c
gcc -Wall -Wstrict-prototypes -O2 -fomit-frame-pointer -c -o tkcond.o
tkcond.c
gcc -Wall -Wstrict-prototypes -O2 -fomit-frame-pointer -c -o tkgen.o tkgen.c
gcc -o tkparse tkparse.o tkcond.o tkgen.o
cat header.tk >> ./kconfig.tk
./tkparse < ../arch/i386/config.in >> kconfig.tk
echo "set defaults \"arch/i386/defconfig\"" >> kconfig.tk
echo "set ARCH \"i386\"" >> kconfig.tk
cat tail.tk >> kconfig.tk
chmod 755 kconfig.tk
make[1]: Leaving directory '/usr/src/linux-2.2.2/scripts'
wish -f scripts/kconfig.tk
```

Then the main xconfig window will appear:

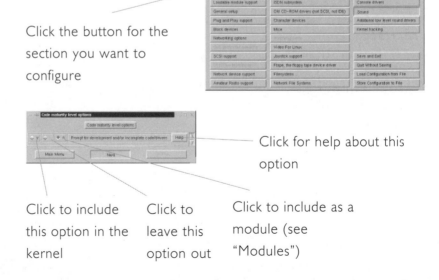

Click the button for the section you want to configure

Click for help about this option

Click to include this option in the kernel

Click to leave this option out

Click to include as a module (see "Modules")

Building the new kernel Ⓢ

When you have finished choosing all the options you want
in the new kernel, you have to save the options and exit the
config program. In xconfig click on the "Save and Exit"
button. In menuconfig select "Exit" then "Yes" in the
following dialog:

Select "Yes" to save
or "No" to abandon
your configuration

| The next stage is to build the list of files which need to
be compiled to make the kernel.

```
make dep
```

2 Next, remove any old files.

```
make clean
```

3 And lastly, build the kernel. This command will take
some time (up to an hour) and will create a
compressed kernel image.

```
make bzImage
```

Modules Ⓢ

Some parts of the kernel, like certain device drivers, are not required all the time from boot-up. In order to save memory, the size of the kernel can be reduced by leaving these items out of the kernel and only loading them when required. This can be done by specifying M for module in the kernel configuration.

Certain items should never be built as modules, for instance support for the ext2 filesystem. If you are going to need continuous use of a kernel function, or you need it at boot time, you should not specify it as a module. Otherwise it is a good idea to specify as many options as you can as modules because the kernel image size will be reduced.

To use modules make sure you enabled "Loadable Module Support" and "Kernel Daemon Support" when you configured the kernel.

Building Modules

When you have configured and built the kernel you need to compile the modules. This is done like this:

1 Build the modules.

```
make modules
```

2 Install the modules in their directories.

```
make modules_install
```

3 Generate module dependency list – so modules which others depend on are loaded correctly.

```
depmod -a
```

To see how to pass parameters to modules see "sound as a module" in the next section.

4 Modules are loaded with "modprobe *modulename*". Unload with "rmmod *modulename*". List loaded modules with "lsmod".

5 Instead of entering "modprobe" it is better to use "kerneld" which should be loaded at boot time. This may be the default for your distribution. When "kerneld" is running it will automatically load and unload modules as needed.

 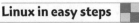

Example: Enabling sound ⓢ

Here you can see a complete example of building the kernel to enable sound in Linux.

1   Change to the "/usr/src/ linux" directory and, as root, enter "make xconfig".

```
#cd /usr/src/linux
#make xconfig
```

2   Find and click on the "Sound configuration" button.

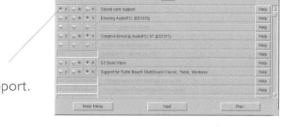

3   Click to enable sound card support.

4   Find your sound card in the list and enable it. Here you can see Sound Blaster enabled.

5   Enter the configuration parameters in the boxes. Find them out from your sound card manual, or if you can boot into Windows look at the properties page in the device manager.

6   To get help on any item click on the button.

7 Click on "Main Menu" on the sound configuration, or "Next" if you want to configure other items.

8 Click "Save and Exit" on the main xconfig menu.

9 Rebuild the kernel.

```
#make dep
#make clean
#make bzImage
```

10 Install and test the new kernel as described on the next page.

Sound as a module

The RedHat version of Linux has a modular sound system. Other distributions can use the standard sound drivers as modules. To pass the parameters to a module you need to add them to the "/etc/conf.modules" file:

Enter the parameters – all on one line.

```
alias sound sb

options sb io=0x220 irq=7 dma=1 dma16=5
mpu_io=0x330
```

To load the module without kerneld use "modprobe sound".

"sb" here means soundblaster–you need to change it to your module. You can find all the modules in the "/lib/modules/X.X.XX/misc" directory. Replace "X.X.XX" with the version of your kernel.

Booting the new Kernel Ⓢ

Once you have built a new Kernel you will need to try it. It is important you don't throw away your old kernel yet as the new one may not be correct.

With Lilo

If you normally use LILO to boot you will need to add a new section to "/etc/lilo.conf". It will look like this:

```
image=/usr/src/Linux/arch/i386/bzImage

   label=new

   root=/dev/hda3

   read-only
```

Enter this to boot the new kernel   New kernel image file

After changing "lilo.conf" you *must* run "lilo" or you won't be able to boot into Linux.

After changing lilo.conf you have to run Lilo to make it take effect. Enter "lilo" at the prompt. When you boot you can now enter "new". This will run the new Kernel. If it works properly you can copy the kernel image file to the usual location and replace your old kernel. Don't forget to run lilo again.

With LoadLin

If you use LoadLin to start Linux from a Windows or DOS session you will have to copy it to your C drive to be able to boot it. The best way to do this is with *mcopy*, part of the Mtools package. Configure Mtools to recognise drive C and use a command like the following:

```
mcopy /usr/src/Linux/arch/i386/bzImage
C:\bzimage.new
```

Then, in Windows or DOS, copy your LINUX.BAT file which contains the LoadLin command to a new file. Change the name of the Kernel file to the one you just copied and test it.

Kernel Upgrading Ⓢ

The kernel can be upgraded either as source or, if a binary package is available for your distribution such as an RPM, simply by installing the new package. This is easier but is less flexible and if you have reconfigured the kernel, you won't have the same configuration after upgrading unless you upgrade the kernel source and build that.

Installing a new kernel source tree

When a new Linux kernel is available the source is made available at *http://www.kernel.org*. This is the main Linux kernel website and contains links to local mirror sites. You might also find the kernel source on a CD-ROM.

The source is normally a gzipped tar package which needs to be uncompressed in the "/usr/src" directory:

1 Copy the tar file to the /usr/src directory and cd to this directory

2 Extract the files

```
tar xvzf linux-2.2.5.tar.gz
```

3 The directory "/usr/src/linux" is a link to the actual kernel source directory. Remake this link for the new version

```
rm linux
ln -s linux-2-2-5 linux
```

Remove the old link

Remake the link for the new version

After upgrading the kernel source you must rebuild and install the new kernel.

Applying a Patch

Because the kernel source is so big, increments in versions are released as patch files, which just contain the differences between the old and the new. To apply a patch, copy the patch file to "/usr/src" and cd to this directory, then apply the patch:

```
bunzip2 patch-2.2.5.bz2
patch < patch-2.2.5
```

Uncompress patch file

Apply patch

Getting On-line Help

In this chapter we will see how to use the on-line manual to find out about Linux commands. You will learn about the Linux HOWTO database and where to get more information when you need it.

Covers

Chapter Fourteen

The man Command

It's easy to get help on any Linux command as the entire manual is on-line, accessible from your hard disk. Included are manual pages for all user commands, system administration commands, file formats and for Linux programmers, run-time library functions and system calls.

To view the entry for a particular command:

1   Enter man *command*

<pre>
man cat
</pre>

2   Press *Return* to scroll up a
line, *space* for next page,
and *q* to quit

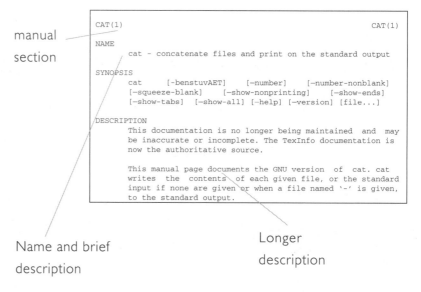

manual
section

```
CAT(1)                                                            CAT(1)

NAME
        cat - concatenate files and print on the standard output

SYNOPSIS
        cat     [-benstuvAET]     [-number]     [-number-nonblank]
        [-squeeze-blank]   [-show-nonprinting]   [-show-ends]
        [-show-tabs]  [-show-all]  [-help]  [-version]  [file...]

DESCRIPTION
        This documentation is no longer being maintained  and  may
        be inaccurate or incomplete. The TexInfo documentation is
        now the authoritative source.

        This manual page documents the GNU version  of  cat. cat
        writes   the   contents  of each given file, or the standard
        input if none are given or when a file named '-' is given,
        to the standard output.
```

Name and brief
description

Longer
description

If you want to search for a word, press / then type the word and press *Return.*

The on-line manuals are organised into 7 sections. The sections are numbered like this:

1	User Commands
2	Kernel system calls
3	Standard library functions
4	Special files
5	File format information
6	Games
7	Miscellaneous
8	System administration commands
9	Non-standard kernel routines

Sometimes an entry appears in more than one section. The full name of a manual entry includes the section number in parentheses, for example *ls(3)*.

When a word has an entry in more than one manual section you can tell the man command which section you want to see by entering the section number before the entry name on the man command.

For example *kill* is both a user command and a system call for programmers. To see the user command enter:

```
man 3 kill
```

For more information about *man* use the command *man man*.

What do you do if you don't know the name of the *man* entry?

Using "man -k *keyword*" will find pages which contain the keyword in their list of keyword entries.

Info pages

Many commands have more information available in the form of "Info" pages. These pages are browsable like man, although more advanced with hyperlinks between sections. In some cases the Info documentation is stated to be more up to date than the corresponding man page, although I have yet to find a man page which contains inaccurate information.

To view an Info page on the cp command enter:

```
info cp
```

If you leave off the command name you will see an introductory page.

Info pages are organised as "nodes". One node is a set of pages about a single topic. You can move through the pages of one node with the following keys:

Space   Next Page

DEL   Previous page

Nodes form a chain with each node, other than the first and last in a chain, having a previous and a next node. Move to the previous node by pressing p and the next by pressing n. Pressing b takes you to the first node in the chain and e the last in the chain.

Some pages contain menus. Menu items appear with an asterisk like this:

```
*Item
```

To select a menu item press m then type the name of the menu item when asked.

You can see a full list of command keys by pressing ? and to quit from the info viewer press q. A tutorial can be seen by pressing h which shows all this in more detail, and you can return to the initial directory page by pressing d.

Getting Quick Help

Sometimes you know the command you want to use but are unable to remember the exact syntax of the command line option to use. For these cases many commands have quick help available which can be viewed by adding "--help" to the command.

For example to display help on the "tar" command:

```
tar --help
```

The command above will show a page or two about the tar (tape archive) command which, despite its name, is the most common command used for creating disk archives on Linux (as well as for making tape archives).

If the help is more than one page you can put it through a "pipe" into the "more" command. Enter it like this:

```
tar --help | more
```

Not all commands support this quick help. Some do support it explicitly, that is using the "--help" option as above. Others don't recognise this option but take the opportunity to show some brief information on usage when they don't understand the option given.

Other commands are less friendly however and do not give any such information.

The Linux HOWTOs

So far we have seen how to get help on particular commands. Sometimes you want to know the details of how to get something done, which might involve several different commands. A good example would be "How do I get Quake running on Linux?"

The HOWTO files, as their name implies, are intended to answer this type of question. Each one shows all the stages necessary to perform a certain task, or the different ways of doing something and gives you the exact commands to do it. You won't learn much about the individual commands used since the HOWTOs are supposed to be used by someone who already knows his or her way around a Linux system and just wants to know the steps involved in getting something potentially complicated to work.

The Quake HOWTO is a good example. It starts by explaining what you need and continues to tell you where you can get Quake. Then it goes into the installation procedure and how to run the various versions of Quake. Then it describes the various options available and so on.

You can see that the HOWTOs are designed to bring together all the little things you need to know to achieve a particular task. In the Quake HOWTO you can find out something about the MesaGL graphics system too, as this is required for one of the versions of Quake.

Other subjects covered include how to run Linux in various foreign languages such as Spanish or Thai; how to use PCMCIA cards with Linux; other types of hardware such as UPS (uninterruptible power supplies) and setting up various services such as a web server or firewall.

HOWTOs are normally provided with your Linux distribution and can be found under the /usr/doc branch. They may be in HTML or plain text format. If you want to get more HOWTOs, or get them in a different format such as Postscript, point your web browser to: http://sunsite.unc.edu/LDP/HOWTO.

Package Documentation

Many packages of software, and programs, come with a complete set of documentation which is installed along with the software on Linux. Sometimes the documentation is good and sometimes it is bad. You can find it in the /usr/doc directory on the system.

Some of this documentation is in plain text format and some is in HTML which will require a browser. You can use the text-based web browser, LYNX, if you do not have a graphical system.

How to read plain text documentation

1 Change to the directory where the files are located

2 Use the `vi` command to view the text files

How to view HTML documents with Lynx

1 Change to the directory where the files are located

2 Use the `lynx` command to view the web pages

In Lynx you can move between "hotlinks" with the up and down arrow keys. Follow one link to another page by pressing the right-arrow key and return using the left-arrow key.

You can get a full list of keys in Lynx by pressing H or ?.

Other Sources of Information

Aside from the many published books covering Linux, the major source of knowledge and information is the Internet. There are two main sources on the net: published documents; and personal communications.

There are documents available for specific software packages, often from the producers of such software but sometimes from third-parties. A search in one of the many Internet search engines will soon find such documentation.

The Linux Documentation Project

Don't forget the website of your Linux distribution for more information, such as:

www.redhat.com
www.suse.com
www.caldera.com
www.debian.org

One of the best places to find published documentation about several different Linux subjects is the Linux Documentation Project. The home address of the LDP is *http://www.metalab.unc.edu/LDP*. The LDP is an independent, non-profit organisation which is the home of the HOWTOs and has produced some excellent freely available books on the following subjects:

- Installation and Getting Started

- Users' guide

- Kernel Programming

News/Mail Lists

The other place to look is on the newsgroups and mailing lists. Newsgroups are accessible with newsreader software and work a little like email, a public forum which anyone can read, and where anyone can post their views (but keep on-topic!). There are several thousand newsgroups on all manner of subjects but try the Linux ones such as comp.os.linux and linux.config

Mailing lists work by email and are a little like newsgroups but more private. You have to subscribe to read or post messages and they tend to be a little more controlled. You can find mailing lists on relevant websites.

Index

D